INVENTING
SCROOGE

THE INCREDIBLE TRUE STORY
BEHIND DICKENS' LEGENDARY
A CHRISTMAS CAROL

BY CARLO DEVITO

CIDER MILL
PRESS

BOOK
PUBLISHERS
KENNEBUNKPORT, MAINE

This book may be ordered by mail from the publisher.
Please include $5.99 for postage and handling.
Please support your local bookseller first!

Books published by Cider Mill Press Book Publishers are available at special discounts for bulk purchases in the United States by corporations, institutions, and other organizations. For more information, please contact the publisher.

Cider Mill Press Book Publishers
"Where good books are ready for press"
12 Spring Street
PO Box 454
Kennebunkport, Maine 04046

Visit us on the Web!
www.cidermillpress.com

Design: Alicia Freile, Tango Media
Typography: Candice Fitzgibbons, Tango Media
Printed in the United States

1 2 3 4 5 6 7 8 9 0

First Edition

This book is dedicated to family. I have been so very, very fortunate to enjoy countless Christmas seasons, none of which would have been worth anything without family. This book is dedicated to my siblings, Claudia, Eugene, and Leigh-Ann; to my aunts and uncles; and to all my cousins . . . you know who you are.

Contents

*"Happy, happy Christmas, that can win us
back to the delusions of our childhood days,
recall to the old man the pleasures of his youth,
and transport the traveler back to his
own fireside and quiet home!"*

—Charles Dickens

Author's Note

The idea of this exercise is not to deconstruct Mr. Dickens' life or work but rather to lift the veil on the creative process. Without question, Charles Dickens remains one of the most widely published and cherished novelists of all time. More than two hundred years after his birth, his popularity has not wavered. And *A Christmas Carol* is arguably his best-known publication thanks to numerous editions of the book, retellings in various print media, dramatic stage performances, and beloved film adaptations. Each time there is a new interpretation, we find another nuance we never suspected. It is an endlessly fascinating story!

It is also not the object of this volume to affect the wonderful reputation that *A Christmas Carol* enjoys. But rather its intent is to see where and how this story came about and how it helped to shape the history of the holiday season in the Western world for more than a century and three quarters, and most likely beyond.

I have only dealt with issues pertaining to the book, and have avoided restating obvious facts about Mr. Dickens' domestic and personal history (except where they influenced the work). It was not my goal to publish a biography of Mr. Dickens (there are too many good ones referenced in this book), but rather to focus on the writer, his process, and his creation.

I also included Mr. Dickens' performances of the work because they were an ongoing part of his creative relationship with the material that he kept reinventing.

That, and like Charles Dickens, I love the holidays.

—*C. DeVito*
January 1, 2014

Prologue

r. Dickens strode out onto the stage of the Tremont Temple Baptist Church.

Originally dubbed the "Temple Theatre" when it opened in 1827, the building was renamed when it was purchased in 1843 by a Baptist group. Throughout its history since, it not only served for religious services but was also utilized for numerous public events such as plays, movies, exhibits, and speeches. The great hall was three stories high, ornate and large. A large number of seats extended out from the proscenium stage, with a solid row of balcony seats ringing the theater.

An Egyptian mummy had been displayed there in September 1850 and was one of the cultural touchstones that year in the city of Boston. Four months later, the Ladies American Home Education Society held one of the largest temperance meetings in the city's history up to that time. The two-thousand-seat auditorium burned down in 1852, but was soon rebuilt. Sam Houston gave a fiery speech against slavery there to a mixed house of white and black abolitionists in February 1855. Five years later a similar group of abolitionists was dispersed from the same theater by the Boston police.

The Tremont Temple Baptist Church in 1851.

And on this day, Bostonians dressed in their holiday best stumbled through the icy winds of winter to see Mr. Dickens perform *A Christmas Carol.* "Just about everyone knows the tale of the miserly Ebenezer Scrooge, who is visited by three ghosts on Christmas Eve, sees the error of his ways, and becomes a jolly benefactor to poor Tiny Tim and his family," reported *The Boston Globe.*

Mr. Dickens' gait was muscular but elegant. He was resplendent in a black, peak-lapelled, double-breasted, three-quarter coat which was unbuttoned so that his glorious and brilliantly colored silk vest shone through. Augmented with a brilliant red cravat and a golden watch fob elegantly draped across his left side, Dickens was the epitome of the dashing Victorian gentleman, elegantly arrayed (and just shy of foppery).

The audience erupted with applause at the mere sight of the famous performer. Placed at the center of the stage was a podium with a small carafe of water and a glass. At its base was a bright cluster of poinsettia plants, red and white. He approached the podium and prepared himself.

"Marley was dead: to begin with. . . . This must be distinctly understood, or nothing wonderful can come of the story I am going to relate," began Mr. Dickens. The crowd went quiet, and the only thing to be heard was his voice.

Mr. Dickens went on for a little less than forty minutes. He gesticulated wildly in some instances, and took great glee in switching from one of the many fantastic characters to another with ease. He changed voices and inflections. He drew laughter along with oohhs and ahhs from the assembled throng. He finished the first half of the presentation to massive applause, which was followed by an intermission.

Charles Dickens first read *A Christmas Carol* to an audience in the United States on December 2, 1867.

It had been his second tour of America after visiting the year before he'd written his great yuletide ghost story. That night, he was an immediate sensation.

But this night, the performer was not Charles Dickens, but rather Gerald Dickens, the great-great-grandson of the famed writer. And here he was in December 2013 reenacting his late ancestor's performance!

Gerald Dickens performing his great-great grandfather's works.

Despite the conveyance of approximately 170 years, the theater was packed to see this reading of one of the most theatrically produced stories in the history of literature. It was Gerald's twentieth year performing the Christmas tale. He had first performed it in 1993, in America, for an event on the 150th anniversary of the story's publication.

"To be honest, I wasn't that keen on doing it, but the event was a charitable one," Gerald told *The Boston Globe* in reference to that first show. "And as soon as I started working on it, it all fell into place. Every major character had their own voice and their own way of standing and their own expression and way of moving and everything else. The further I worked through the story, the more it came together. It was an amazing experience."

Over the years he has performed up to thirty dates per year, both in the US and the UK. "I can be exhausted and feeling like the last thing I want to do is dragging myself onstage and performing, and yet as soon as you say, 'Marley was dead: to begin with,' everything just kicks in and you can't help yourself," he continued. "I don't know where that energy comes from, but the text seems to generate it."

The second half of the performance continued and the audience was just as rapt by the unfolding story. Finally, he ended the story of the reclamation of Ebenezer Scrooge, "and it was always said of him, that he knew how to keep Christmas well, if any man alive possessed the knowledge. May that be truly said of us, and all of us! And so, as Tiny Tim observed, God bless us, every one!" The crowd roared with applause as they rose to give Mr. Dickens a standing ovation.

Audiences have been applauding this tale since it was first published during the Christmas season more than a century and a half ago, and those enthusiastic cheers will surely continue for many years to come.

This enduring story of a covetous old sinner who has lost touch with his humanity has moved generations of readers worldwide; it has been translated into countless languages and transformed into numerous stage productions and cinematic adaptations over the years. At its core, A Christmas Carol delivers a timeless message of hope; it's about how each one of us can be saved, and about how we can redeem ourselves annually with the help of our friends, family, and loved ones

Yet most inspiring of all is the story behind the story: the incredible true story of how Dickens came to write this legendary yuletide tale.

The Train Ride

arly in the morning on Wednesday, October 4, 1843, Charles Dickens left his family and his dwellings on 1 Devonshire Terrace, near Regents Park, and hailed a hackney cab. He was just going to nearby Euston Station, but he had luggage because his train ride would take him a long way off, if only for a short period.

"There is a hackney-coach stand under the very window at which we are writing; there is only one coach on it now, but it is a fair specimen of the class of vehicles to which we have alluded—a great, lumbering, square concern of a dingy yellow color (like a bilious brunette), with very small glasses, but very large frames; the panels are ornamented with a faded coat of arms, in shape something like a dissected bat, the axletree is red, and the majority of the wheels are green," Dickens once wrote.

"The horses, with drooping heads, and each with a mane and tail as scanty and straggling as those of a worn-out rocking-horse, are standing patiently on some damp straw, occasionally wincing, and rattling the harness; and now and then, one of them lifts his mouth to the ear of his companion, as if he were saying, in a whisper, that he should like to assassinate the coachman. The coachman himself is in the watering-house; and the waterman, with his hands forced into his pockets as far as they can possibly go, is dancing the 'double shuffle,' in front of the pump, to keep his feet warm."

The cab wheeled about and Dickens got in. The horses popped and clicked, and the coach bounced up and down as it made its way over the uneven streets. No matter the final destination, Dickens was preoccupied with his recent disappointments. He stopped thinking of them for a moment, and checked once again to see if he had his speech with him. Yes, it was there. In those days, Dickens, then thirty-one years old, was not yet the grand man of letters, but a young writer still possibly better known by the masses as "Boz" than by his real name. But Charles Dickens' name was well known in the book trade, and he was a London favorite thanks to his string of successes—*The Pickwick Papers, Nicholas Nickleby, The Old Curiosity Shop,* and *Oliver Twist,* among others.

Charles Dickens as Boz.

But then there was his trip to America, and his subsequent work *American Notes*, and then his next book *Martin Chuzzlewit*.

"*Chuzzlewit* had fallen short of all the expectations formed of it in regard to sale," wrote close friend and biographer John Forster. "By much the most masterly of his writings hitherto, the public had rallied to it in far less numbers than to any of its predecessors . . . whatever the causes, here was the undeniable fact of a grave depreciation of sale in his writings, unaccompanied by any falling off either in themselves or in the writer's reputation." *Martin Chuzzlewit* had sold less than a third of the sales of his previous bestsellers.

"It is not uncommon though, for a novelist to lose part of his audience as he grows more ambitious," wrote Jane Smiley, a bestselling author herself, on Dickens' perplexing sales of *Chuzzlewit*. "The willingness, even the ability, of the audience to follow a favorite writer into work of greater complexity and more somber vision isn't always immediate, and every author whose sole income is from his writings has to reckon with this dilemma."

Dickens was arguing with his publishers over the original advance, which was now still very much unearned, and there was discussion of the return of some of those advanced monies. But with a growing family, and a desire to be firmly ensconced in the middle class (no mean feat for a writer then), Dickens was deeply concerned about finances. Instead of bolstering his monetary situation, *Chuzzlewit* might now be his ruination.

Dickens probably scheduled the 10 a.m. from Euston Station of the London and Birmingham Railway. That train reached Birmingham by 2:45 p.m., and then promptly arrived in Manchester at 6:25 p.m. just in time for dinner. The trip was 197.5 miles according to the schedule of the day.

Euston Station was the first intercity railway station in London. It opened on July 20, 1837, as the terminus of the London and Birmingham Railway. By the time Dickens approached Euston Station, it had become the hub of the London and North Western Railway. With its massive Doric columns and classic triangular façade, it looked more like a Greek temple than a train station. It had a 200-foot-long train shed and only two platforms—one for departures and one for arrivals. The station was continually expanding as rail traffic grew, until the great hall of the station was finally completed in 1849.

The site had been selected in the early 1830s by George and Robert Stephenson, engineers of the London and Birmingham Railway. The area was then mostly farmland at the edge of the expanding city of London, and the railroad company had had to overcome strenuous objections by local farmers to begin construction. The station was named after Euston Hall in Suffolk, the ancestral home of the Dukes of Grafton who were the main landowners in the area.

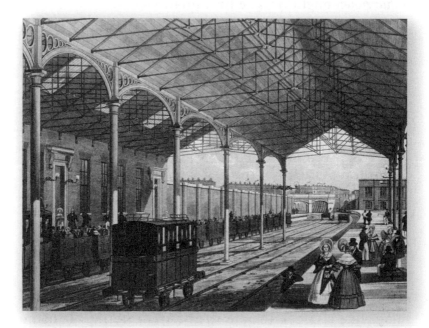

Euston Station in 1837.

Dickens described the building of the London and Birmingham Railroad, writing, "Houses were knocked down, streets broken through and stopped; deep pits and trenches dug, in the ground; enormous heaps of earth and clay thrown up; buildings that were undermined and shaken, propped by great beams. Here, a chaos of carts, overthrown and jumbled together, lay topsy-turvy at the bottom of a steep unnatural hill; there, confused treasurers of iron soaked and rusted in something that had accidentally become a pond. Everywhere were bridges that led nowhere . . . and piles of scaffolding, and wilderness of brick, and giant forms of cranes, and tripods straddling above nothing. . . . Boiling water hissed and heaved with dilapidated walls; whence, also, the glare and roar of flames came issuing forth; and mounds of ashes blocked up rights of way, and wholly changed the law and custom of the neighborhood."

But Dickens loved the railway terminus, and about his regular nighttime walks once wrote, ". . . when I wanted variety, a railway terminus with the morning mails coming in, was remunerative company. But like most of the company to be had in this world, it lasted only a very short time. The station lamps would burst out ablaze, the porters would emerge from places of concealment, the cabs and trucks would rattle to their places (the post-office carts were already in theirs), and, finally, the bell would strike up, and the train would come banging in. But there were few passengers and little luggage, and everything scuttled away with the greatest expedition. The locomotive post-offices, with their great nets—as if they had been dragging the country for bodies—would fly open as to their doors, and would disgorge a smell of lamp, an exhausted clerk, a guard in a red coat, and their bags of letters; the engine would blow and heave and perspire, like an engine wiping its forehead and saying what a run it had had; and within ten minutes the lamps were out, and I was . . . alone again."

A porter took Dickens' things and the two wound their way through the station to the departure terminal. Dickens had already acquired his trademark look of parted, longish, dark and wild hair, and a beard of varying length. He was relatively trim, though he was not tall. He may have worn a gray suit, but probably wore one of his renowned brightly colored vests and an equally shocking cravat for a splash of color.

His walk was crisp and deliberate. He was an avid walker who likely walked up to twenty miles a day. "I think I must be the descendant, at no great distance, of some irreclaimable tramp," Dickens once said of himself. On these long walks, Dickens exhibited what his walking friends once described as his "swinging" gait. He also "made a practice of increasing his speed when ascending a hill," according to his friend Marcus Stone.

Dickens kept his hat low upon his brow, and his gaze, which naturally went straight out as he was a wonderful observer of things, darted toward the floor. At this time Dickens was becoming a celebrity, and he had already come to realize that with his newfound fame he had lost the right to be a private citizen. More than once he'd had to change rooms in a hotel, or change hotels completely, to avoid the frenzy of people trying to meet him, shake his hand, etc. Dickens wanted fame, but the crowds could prove unruly. This morning, he just wanted to get on the train.

Dickens ascended into the coach and waited for the train to pull out. He was joined by his friend Thomas Mitton, who had once been his schoolmate. Both had been law clerks together, and after Mitton became a solicitor Dickens hired him for representation. The two chatted as friends do, and may have shared newspapers, magazines, and journals. It would be a long ride.

Maybe one of them had a copy of the newest publication, the *News of the World*, which had published its first issue that month. Certainly news was still coming out of Greece about the uprising in that country the month before on September 3. Or possibly Mitton might have had the September 28 issue of *The Economist*, another new journal. The election of the Lord Mayor of London was in its final days, as workmen busily fitted out Guildhall for the Lord Mayor's Banquet. And of course there was great fascination with Burgess, a clerk in the power-of-attorney office at the Bank of England, who had recently absconded with more than £8,000.

Dickens was vexed. He was heading to Manchester to give a speech along with Benjamin Disraeli and Richard Cobden. Disraeli was an accomplished novelist turned politician, having gained a seat in Parliament; he would later become prime minister. Cobden was also a Member of Parliament and had cofounded the Anti-Corn Law League to fight against the law that helped wealthy landowners by imposing high tariffs on imported wheat, which in turn drove up the average cost of bread; at the same time, industry and business owners were trying to lower average workers' wages.

All three were supposed to speak at the Manchester Athenaeum, an organization which provided the working class with education and culture in an effort to better their lives. Dickens himself had grown absolutely resolute in his position that an educated working class would be a benefit to both themselves as well as the nation.

Dickens had a profound concern for the working class, and especially the countless exploited children who had been forced to work in factories at a young age. Charles' father, John Dickens, was forced by his creditors into the Marshalsea debtors' prison in Southwark, London, in 1824. Charles had taken a job just two weeks before his father was sent to Marshalsea. He worked and pawned his mother's jewelry and family furniture in a local shop on Hampstead Road, not far from the Euston train shed, where he became well known until they had run out of things to sell. His mother and the youngest children then joined John Dickens at Marshalsea (a common occurrence in those days). Charles, then twelve years old, boarded with Elizabeth Roylance, a family friend, at 112 College Place, Camden Town. According to Dickens, she was "a reduced [impoverished] old lady, long known to our family." Dickens was forced to work in a boot black factory labeling pots of boot black six days a week, from 8 a.m. to 8 p.m., for six shillings a week, and was allowed to visit with his family at Marshalsea on Sundays. Child laborers, as he had once been forced to experience first-hand, suffered immensely from ignorance and want.

The courtyard at Marshalsea Prison.

"Dickens lived in what in effect was a slum—Camden Town in north London, cramped, damp, depressing, shrouded in smog and fog of what he called 'a great and dirty city'," wrote actor and scholar Simon Callow. "He now descended into hell, working a ten hour work day, engaged in the most menial of tasks, in the most sordid of conditions, surrounded by the roughest of working companions. He was tormented by the loss of his former happiness, and by the collapse of his dreams of growing up to be a learned and distinguished man."

"His schoolboy's few clothes became increasingly shabby and he detested the difficult-to-remove and defiling polish that grimed his hands and fingernails. As an adult he would be obsessive about his cleanliness. He would also be fetishistic about his clothes, from the dandy splendor of his twenties and thirties to the elegant seriousness of his later dress," wrote biographer Fred Kaplan more than a century later.

Now, amongst the papers he had with him was his speech, which in part read, "And this I know, that the first unpurchasable blessing earned by every man who makes an effort to improve himself in such a place as the Athenaeum, is self-respect—an inward dignity of character, which, once acquired and righteously maintained, nothing—no, not the hardest drudgery, nor the direst poverty—can vanquish. Though he should find it hard for a season even to keep the wolf—hunger—from his door, let him but once have chased the dragon—ignorance—from his hearth, and self-respect and hope are left him. You could no more deprive him of those sustaining qualities by loss or destruction of his worldly goods, than you could, by plucking out his eyes, take from him an internal consciousness of the bright glory of the sun."

But Dickens was flummoxed. He had given speeches before but he was never really sure of their effectiveness. Was this the best way to reach people on the subject? How could he be more convincing? He had thought to publish a pamphlet on this same subject, but wondered what effect such a publication might have.

The train lurched forward. Until 1844 trains were pulled up the incline to Camden Town by cables because the London and Birmingham Railway's Act of Parliament prohibited the use of locomotives in the Euston area, a long-lasting gift to the contentious farmers who'd lost their battle with the railroad.

Going north, as he passed Camden Town, Dickens could not help but wince. There was the old neighborhood of his youth, when his family had moved to London, where the old house was. As he looked out to the right, passing Delancey Street, he gazed up that road for a brief instant, remembering the left-hand turn onto Bayham Street, to the tiny house where he and his mother and father and six brothers and sisters lived all packed together, while his father squandered money he didn't have and tried to support his family on a clerk's salary.

Those were dark times for Dickens. And while his current circumstances were worrisome due to the disappointing sales of *Chuzzlewit*, he was still far away from there in many ways. But his memories of Camden Town were never pleasant and seemed never far away. They were more like a lurking ghost, looming always like hunger at the door.

Wrote biographer Claire Tomalin, "All of these experiences—of debt, fear, angry creditors, bailiffs, pawnbrokers, prison, living in freezing empty rooms and managing on what can be borrowed or begged—were impressed on his mind and used again and again in his stories and novels, sometimes grimly, sometimes with humor."

The train rumbled toward the Birmingham train station, used by passenger trains between 1838 and 1854 when it was the terminus for both the London and Birmingham Railway and the Grand Junction Railway. This was the halfway point of Dickens' train ride. With its Doric columns, grand arches, and four platforms, Birmingham (later name Curzon Street Station) was a bustling railway hub.

The sluggish sales of *Martin Chuzzlewit* ate at Dickens. He did not understand its failure. Was his career at an end?

His friend and biographer Forster tried to explain it by way of saying, "The primary cause of this, there is little doubt, had been the change to weekly issues in the form of publication of his last two stories; for into everything in this world mere habit enters more largely than we are apt to suppose. Nor had the temporary withdrawal to

America been favorable to an immediate resumption by his readers of their old and intimate relations. This also is to be added, that the excitement by which a popular reputation is kept up to the highest selling mark, will always be subject to lulls too capricious for explanation."

"I am so irritated, so rubbed in the tenderest part of my eyelids with bay-salt," wrote Dickens to Forster, "that a wrong kind of fire is burning in my head, and I don't think I *can* write. Nevertheless . . . I am bent on paying the money." Dickens was fuming, but he wasn't completely unhinged. Always a smart businessman, he asked Forster to sound out Bradbury and Evans, a printer, before axing Chapman and Hall. Though Forster and Mitton were both friends of Dickens, the two did not like each other. But it is sure that Dickens and Mitton must have spent some time talking on this point.

Dickens was distraught and frustrated, later writing to Forster, "You know, as well as I, that I think *Chuzzlewit* is in a hundred points immeasurably the best of my stories. That I feel my power now, more than I ever did. That I have a greater confidence in myself than I ever had. That I know, if I have health, I could sustain my place in the minds of thinking men, though fifty writers started up tomorrow. But how many readers do not think! How many take it upon trust from knaves and idiots, that one writes too fast, or runs a thing to death! How coldly did this very book go on for months, until it forced itself up in people's opinion, without forcing itself up in sale! If I wrote for forty thousand Forsters, or for forty thousand people who know I write because I can't help it, I should have no need to leave the scene. But this very book warns me that if I can leave it for a time, I had better do so, and must do so."

Money was in the forefront of Dickens mind. His wife Catherine was with child. The baby would be due in January. Dickens was by all accounts a wonderful father, but he was already vexed, for his household had grown quickly. They already had four children, and now with the fifth there would be nurses to pay, the visitation of the mother-in-law, and the providing for of the other children as well. This new mouth to feed, while of course a joyous blessing, must have seemed yet another layer of expense in Dickens' eyes.

While visiting Broadstairs, a vacation home popular with Dickens and his family near the shore, he awoke from a dream one night during the summer just past. The dream stuck with Dickens, and plagued him.

Famed biographer Peter Ackroyd wrote of it, "This was a dream, also, in which his apparent frustration at the fact that Catherine was about to have another child, thus adding to his already large family's demands, is expressed in the image of a baby being skewered on a toasting fork. The dream stayed with him . . . his own feeling of helplessness and indebtedness are strangely allied with his reaction to the children of the ragged school and the laboring men of Manchester Athenaeum. So it is that the public concerns and the private fantasies come together in a complete statement."

Dickens thought of his sister, Fanny, who now lived in Manchester. Fanny amongst all his brothers and sisters was his favorite. She was two years older than Charles. Dickens held fond memories of their days spent together with their father, John Dickens, on the navy pay yacht in Chatham. They would run about the deck and watch the shore and the seagulls as the small vessel made its way up to Medway and Sheerness. On the way they would see two naval prison ships, *Eurylis* and *Canada*, and the hospital ship *Hercules*.

The two had attended an old dame school (a pejorative name for a school run by an elderly lady who it was presumed knew how to read and write), which was set above an odorous dyer's shop. Dickens later remembered the school for the woman who ran it with a birch stick. Fanny was Dickens' confidante and conspirator in childhood. The two became bonded, and Dickens was in love with his sister (in a strictly platonic way) for the rest of his life. And she, too, was devoted to him.

It was Fanny whom he would visit by 9 a.m. on Sunday morning at the school, and then the two of them would go to Marshalsea. In 1823 Fanny had been accepted at the Royal Academy of Music in Hanover Square. She studied with a former pupil of Ludwig van Beethoven, Ignaz Moscheles.

This was not an inexpensive education, at thirty-eight guineas a year, especially for a family reeling from debt. And it may be supposed that Dickens' own education had been scuttled as a consequence of Fanny's gift for music.

Fanny had gained a kind of notoriety in Charles' eyes when she performed on June 29, 1824, at a public concert which was attended by Princess Augusta, the sister of King George IV. The younger Dickens was struck by the experience, recalling years later, "I could not bear to think of myself—beyond the reach of all such honorable emulation and success. The tears ran down my face. I felt as if my heart were rent. I prayed, when I went to bed that night, to be lifted out of the humiliation and neglect in which I was. I had never suffered so much before. . . . "

Despite this episode, Fanny held Charles' heartstrings as a boy and young man. By 1834 she was a gifted singer and gave public concerts. She had been awarded an associate honorary membership at the Royal Academy. Catherine Hogarth, Charles' soon-to-be wife, had described Fanny as "a very pretty girl who sings beautifully." In 1837, though, she married fellow musician Henry Burnett and the couple moved to Manchester. Fanny had given up her career in 1839 after the birth of her son Harry Burnett, who was physically disabled. According to literary historians Michael and Mollie Hardwick, Fanny "helped [her husband] in the training of the choir at Rusholme Road Congregational Chapel."

Despite the fact that Charles was not terribly fond of Henry, seeing Fanny was always a treat. In fact, it may be supposed that the only reason he accepted the present engagement to speak was based on the opportunity to visit with his sister.

Fanny Dickens.

And while Dickens visited Manchester numerous times in his life, he had mixed feelings for the town itself. He later wrote of it, as "Coketown," in *Hard Times*: "It was a town of red brick, or a brick that would have been red if the smoke and ashes would have allowed it . . . a town of machinery and tall chimneys, out of which interminable serpents of smoke trailed themselves forever and ever, and never got uncoiled. It had a black canal in it, and a river that ran purple with some ill-smelling dye."

After arriving at Liverpool Road Station in Manchester, the two friends parted. Dickens then made his way to a suburb of Manchester named Higher Ardwick, and Mitton departed for a hotel in Manchester. Dickens refused to stay in a local hotel, "not caring to be under hourly observation." Instead he stayed with Fanny. "The Burnetts lived in one of the dignified Georgian houses in Upper Brook Street, behind Oxford Road," wrote Michael and Mollie Hardwick.

There was a small gathering at the Burnetts' that night. One of the attendees was Sir E. W. Watkin, First Baronet, a well-known Member of Parliament and a railway baron to boot. Mitton came as well.

"We were indebted for the presence of Charles Dickens to the kind influence of his elder sister—Mrs. Burnett— a self-denying saint, if ever one existed," wrote Watkin.

"I shall enforce the necessity and usefulness of education," Dickens told the group, according to Watkin. "I must give it to them strong."

The one person Dickens did wish to see was Rev. William Giles, the schoolteacher of his youth in those idyllic days before the move to London (and eventually Camden Town) that Dickens still daydreamed about. It was thought that Giles had attended some classes at Oxford. His school focused on letter-writing and composition. Dickens remembered the school fondly, especially its fields where the boys played sports and acted out heroic feats. Giles was a helper, a teacher, and a guide for Dickens in the best of all possible ways that a teacher can be, and Dickens remained fond of him for the rest of his life. He was one of those adults who bent down to help a young child, in Dickens' eyes.

The next day was the gala itself. Disraeli and Cobden were up on the stage with Dickens. All three gave rousing speeches. Dickens railed against the want of education in England at that time, saying that day upon the stage, "How often have we heard from a large class of men wise in their generation, who would really seem to be born and bred for no other purpose than to pass into currency counterfeit and mischievous scraps of wisdom, as it is the sole pursuit of some other criminals to utter base coin—how often have we heard from them, as an all-convincing argument, that 'a little learning is a dangerous thing?' Why, a little hanging was considered a very dangerous thing, according to the same authorities, with this difference, that, because a little hanging was dangerous, we had a great deal of it; and, because a little learning was dangerous, we were to have none at all. Why, when I hear such cruel absurdities gravely reiterated, I do sometimes begin to doubt whether the parrots of society are not more pernicious to its interests than its birds of prey. I should be glad to hear such people's estimate of the comparative danger of 'a little learning' and a vast amount of ignorance; I should be glad to know which they consider the most prolific parent of misery and crime . . . I should be glad to assist them in their calculations, by carrying them into certain gaols and nightly refuges I know of, where my own heart dies within me, when I see thousands of immortal creatures condemned, without alternative or choice, to tread, not what our great poet calls the 'primrose path' to the everlasting bonfire, but one of jaded flints and stones, laid down by brutal ignorance, and held together, like the solid rocks, by years of this most wicked axiom."

It was, according to Dickens' friend Forster, "a matter always nearest his heart, the education of the very poor. He protested against the danger of calling a little learning dangerous."

Dickens concluded his speech, saying, "I am quite certain that long after your institution, and others of the same nature, have crumbled into dust, the noble harvest of the seed sown in them will shine out brightly in the wisdom, the mercy, and the forbearance of another race."

"The soiree of the next evening was brilliant. Dickens was at his very best; and it must have been difficult indeed to follow so admirable a speaker. But Mr. Disraeli certainly shared the honors and the applause of this great meeting. His speech, in fact, created so decided a sensation that I was asked to invite him to preside at the soiree of the coming year of 1844—which he did.

The gala over, Dickens was restless, and after much fanfare he took a long walk around Manchester. He kept turning over the speeches of the night in his head, and was plagued by the simple fact that getting his point across speech by speech was a nice effort, but not effective.

"Something about 'the bright eyes and beaming faces' on which he had looked down at the Manchester Athenaeum had given him the inspiration for a glowing, heart-moving story in which he would appeal to people's essential humanity," wrote famed British literary lion Edgar Johnson.

Indeed, Dickens had recently taken an interest in Ragged Schools. Ragged Schools were charitable schools dedicated to the free education of destitute children in nineteenth century Britain. The schools were developed in working-class districts of the rapidly expanding industrial towns. They provided free education, food, clothing, lodging, and other home missionary services for these children. Working in the poorest districts, teachers (who were often local working people) initially utilized stables, lofts, and railway arches for their classes. There was an emphasis on reading, writing, arithmetic, and study of the Bible.

According to Forster, the original schools were "begun by a shoemaker of Southampton and a chimney-sweep of Windsor." In 1843, Charles Dickens began his association with the schools and visited the Field Lane Ragged School. He was appalled by the conditions, yet moved toward reform.

Dickens wrote some time later, "This attempt is being made in certain of the most obscure and squalid parts of the Metropolis, where rooms are opened, at night, for the gratuitous instruction of all comers, children or adults, under the title of RAGGED SCHOOLS. The name implies the purpose. They who are too ragged, wretched, filthy, and forlorn, to enter any other place: who could gain admission into no charity school, and who would be driven from any church door; are invited to come in here, and find some people not depraved, willing to teach them something, and show them some sympathy, and stretch a hand out, which is not the iron hand of Law, for their correction."

While he initially intended to write a pamphlet on the plight of poor children, Dickens realized that a dramatic story would have more impact.

All this turned in the head of Dickens as he walked the streets, as was his custom, late, late at night. How to get the story across? The next day, he boarded the train once again and took the daylong journey back to London. All the discussions, all the people he had met, now swirled in his head. A story, a story, but how to tell it? Something began to take shape in Dickens' mind. A story was stirring. Characters were beginning to form. But who would be the protagonist? The point of the story was clear to him. The lesson, the moral, the theme were already in place. But the story. Dickens turned it over in his head. . . .

With *Chuzzlewitt* droning on, or so it seemed, something different had to be written.

Wrote Forster years later, "Active as he had been in the now ending year, and great as were its varieties of employment; his genius in its highest mood, his energy unwearied in good work, and his capacity for enjoyment without limit; he was able to signalize its closing months by an achievement supremely fortunate, which but for disappointments the year had also brought might never have been thought of. He had not begun until a week after his return from Manchester, where the fancy first occurred to him, and before the end of November he had finished, his memorable *Christmas Carol.*"

Stave I

Ebenezer Scrooge

*Scrooge! A squeezing, wrenching, grasping, scraping,
covetous, old sinner!*

ickens returned from Manchester and continued
to be intrigued by the story that was swirling in
his mind. He walked the streets of London as he
pieced together the story and the plot. From October
through November, Dickens walked many, many nights,
often not embarking until after dark, and sometimes
returning well into the morning hours of the clock's dial.

Dickens eventually wrote of his combination of
insomnia and restlessness, explaining, "Some years ago,
a temporary inability to sleep, referable to a distressing
impression, caused me to walk about the streets all

night, for a series of several nights. The disorder might have taken a long time to conquer, if it had been faintly experimented on in bed; but, it was soon defeated by the brisk treatment of getting up directly after lying down, and going out, and coming home tired at sunrise." He continued, "In the course of those nights, I finished my education in a fair amateur experience of houselessness. My principal object being to get through the night, the pursuit of it brought me into sympathetic relations with people who have no other object every night in the year."

"None of Dickens characters knew London as well as the novelist himself. No one walked its high roads and its streets and lanes as much, and as avidly, as he did. His fascination with the city, it thoroughfares and its by-ways was established early in his life. London scenes seemed to have inspired him," wrote Dickens scholar Andrew Sanders.

"The restlessness of a great city, and the way in which it tumbles and tosses before it can get to sleep, formed one of the first entertainments offered to the contemplation of us houseless people. It lasted about two hours. We lost a great deal of companionship when the late public-houses turned their lamps out, and when the potmen thrust the last brawling drunkards into the street; but stray vehicles and stray people were left us, after that. If we were very lucky, a policeman's rattle sprang and a fray turned up; but, in general, surprisingly little of this diversion was provided. Except in the Haymarket, which is the worst kept part of London, and about Kent-street in the Borough, and along a portion of the line of the Old Kent-road, the peace was seldom violently broken," Dickens remarked. "After all seemed quiet, if one cab rattled by, half-a-dozen would surely follow; and Houselessness even observed that intoxicated people appeared to be magnetically attracted towards each other; so that we knew when we saw one drunken object staggering against the shutters of a shop, that another drunken object would stagger up before five minutes were out, to fraternise or fight with it. When we made a divergence from the regular species of drunkard, the thin-armed, puff-faced, leaden-lipped gin-drinker, and encountered a rarer specimen of a more decent appearance, fifty to one but that specimen was dressed in soiled mourning. As the street experience in the night, so the street experience in the day; the common folk who come unexpectedly into a little property, come unexpectedly into a deal of liquor."

"For Dickens, London was a city not of dark contrasts, but of an extraordinary variety and energy. From the very beginning of his career as a writer he knew he had a distinctive vocation, and that vocation was to articulate the phenomena that was London," wrote Dickens scholar Andrew Sanders.

Dickens wanted something magical, fairy-like, with supernatural elements and the like. He must have thought back to a story he had told inside the larger book of

The Pickwick Papers. His new story would reimagine that of the character Gabriel Grubb in the chapter "The Story of the Goblins Who Stole a Sexton." In that story, Grubb, a gravedigger, was determined not to make merry at Christmas time. Grubb was kidnapped by goblins and convinced to change his ways. Dickens wanted something that used this story but fit his philosophical ideas on economics and humanity toward man. But the basic principle appealed to him. He would use horror, memory, and a touch of fairy dust to concoct this new, more modern parable.

These kinds of stories were not new to literature. Men confronting demons or angels were popular literary backwaters, with stories like "The Devil and Tom Walker" by Washington Irving, wherein a miserly old man makes a deal with the devil. While he becomes very rich, he cannot save himself, and eventually death comes in black garments to take him away. Dickens was a fan of Irving and sure knew of the story. There had been many of these, most of them owing their origins of the old German legend of Faust.

One of the thoughts that occurred to him was using the concept of a Christmas carol as his overriding theme, with the book broken up into 'staves.' The word 'stave' in the world of music is actually a term for verse, stanza, or a metrical unit of a poem. It an ancient form of verse or a stanza of a song. Staves are traditionally known as the pieces of a barrel that fit together closely.

The idea of calling it "A *Christmas Carol*" seems to have been first and foremost upon his mind. And he kept to the idea that it would be shaped like a carol in structure. Popular carols of the day were "God Rest Ye Merry Gentlemen" (which dated back to the mid-1700s), "O Christmas Tree" (1824), "The Holly and the Ivy" (fifteenth and sixteenth century), and "Adeste Fideles" (which was later translated into "O Come, All Ye Faithful" in 1841).

Several carols are usually used in productions of the story in modern times which actually were written after *Carol's* publication, including "Good King Wenceslas" (1853), "I Heard the Bells on Christmas Day" (Henry Wadsworth Longfellow, 1863), "We Three Kings of Orient Are" (1863), and "Deck the Halls" (a sixteenth century Welsh tune not translated to English until 1862).

Armed with this, Dickens decided to use the word "stave" instead of "staff"—possibly because the idea was that the pieces all fit snuggly like a barrel, watertight—to increase the sense of construction as a small, self-contained story.

Now Dickens began to turn the story over in his head, and he searched through his notebooks for ideas and clues that would unlock the tale. He decided to tell the story of the reclamation of a covetous old sinner, and he had the perfect character. But first he had to find his diary of a previous year. Therein lay the first and most important lock. In that diary he had written down the name he knew he was destined to use.

In 1841 Dickens had visited Edinburgh, Scotland. Friend Forster received "[h]is first letter from Edinburgh, where he and Mrs. Dickens had taken up quarters at the Royal Hotel on their arrival the previous night."

"I have been this morning to the Parliament House, and am now introduced (I hope) to everybody in Edinburgh. The hotel is perfectly besieged, and I have been forced to take refuge in a sequestered apartment at the end of a long passage, wherein I write this letter," Dickens wrote to Forster on June 23, 1841. "They talk of 300 at the dinner. We are very well off in point of rooms, having a handsome sitting-room, another next to it for Clock purposes, a spacious bedroom, and large dressing-room adjoining. The castle is in front of the windows, and the view noble. There was a supper ready last night which would have been a dinner anywhere," remarked Dickens.

"This was his first practical experience of the honors his fame had won for him, and it found him as eager to receive as all were eager to give," concluded Forster.

While in Edinburgh, Dickens, looking to kill time during one of his walks, visited the Canongate Kirkyard (Churchyard) around Canongate Kirk on the Royal Mile in Edinburgh, Scotland. The churchyard was used for burials from the late 1680s until the mid-twentieth century. The most celebrated burials at the kirkyard were the economist Adam Smith and the Scottish poet Robert Fergusson. But while walking through the grave-yard, Dickens noticed an odd sight—the tombstone of Ebenezer Lennox Scroggie.

In the gloaming of an evening in the capital, assisted by an episode of mild dyslexia, Charles Dickens created one of literature's most famous characters. Scroggie's tombstone read "meal man," but through his misreading Dickens interpreted the inscription as "mean man." He later scribbled in his notebook, "To be remembered through eternity only for being mean seemed the greatest testament to a life wasted."

Canongate Kirk in Edinburgh, Scotland.

A year or two later, Dickens pulled this name up out of his notebook and, in changing it to Ebenezer Scrooge, had finally found the right sinner for his tale. One cannot

be sure today why Dickens changed the name, but coin-
cidentally, the now obscure English verb "scrouge" meant
to squeeze or press, and Dickens used those words to
describe Scrooge.

"According to Peter Clark, a British political economist who seems the starting point for this story, Dickens
misread the inscription. It actually said 'Meal man,'
because Scroggie was a corn merchant," reported the
broadsheet *The Scotsman*. "Scroggie was far from being
the Scrooge of the story being somewhat licentious by
nature, tupping at least one servant over a gravestone
and into pregnancy, goosing a Countess at the General
Assembly of the Church of Scotland and in general
enjoying the good things in this life while there was time
to do so. And, of course, as a corn merchant he saved
and improved far more lives than anyone just giving away
their money does, as his Great Uncle (Adam Smith)
points out in Book IV, Chapter 5 (start at para 40) of
the *Wealth of Nations*." Through his mother, Scroggie was
the great-nephew of the eighteenth-century political
economist and philosopher Adam Smith.

Of course, while this mistake yielded one of fiction's
most revered characters, Scroggie himself was one of
Scotland's greatest characters. For it was true that Scroggie
was a sinner, and he was covetous, but not of money.
For Scroggie was a most successful businessman and a well-
known hedonist who loved wine, women, and parties.

Scroggie was born in Kirkcaldy, Fife, date unknown. And he was buried in Edinburgh in 1836. The grave marker was lost during construction work on part of the kirkyard in 1932. "Ebenezer Scroggie was a successful merchant, vintner and Town Councillor (or Baillie) in Edinburgh. He held the first contract to supply whisky to the Royal Navy in Leith and was also responsible for supplying the drink for King George IV's visit to Edinburgh in 1822. This alone would have moved him into the 'Fortune 500' if such a concept had existed at the time," reported historum.com. "Scroggie was known as a dandy and terrible philanderer who had several sexual liaisons which made him the talk of the town. He was a jovial and kindly man, not the mean-spirited miser with which he was associated."

It would seem that while Scroggie and Scrooge were both sinners, one had more fun than the other.

External heat and cold had little influence on Scrooge. No warmth could warm, no wintry weather chill him. No wind that blew was bitterer than he, no falling snow was more intent upon its purpose, no pelting rain less open to entreaty. Foul weather didn't know where to have him.

So, Ebenezer Scrooge now had a name, and Dickens had an idea of what he wanted him to be like, but who was Scrooge in Dickens' mind? Who were the Scrooges of the world at that time? Who would give Scrooge his voice?

Dickens turned to men he loathed. He turned to men with whom he violently disagreed. There were several men whom Dickens used to put words into Scrooge's mouth. He based the miserly part of Scrooge's character on a noted British eccentric and miser named John Elwes (1714–1789), and it is popularly thought that Scrooge's opinions and comments on the poor of London were based on those of demographer and political economist Thomas Malthus.

John Elwes (a.k.a. "Elwes the Miser") was born April 7, 1714, and died November 26, 1789. He was a Member of Parliament for Berkshire (1772–1784) and a noted eccentric and miser. He was thought to have inspired characters in several novels during the period following his death, including Dickens' *Our Mutual Friend* and John Scarfe's *The Miser's Daughter*.

His birth name was "John Elwes Meggot," and he was born into a respectable English family. His father, Robert Meggot, was a Southwark brewer and his grandfather Sir George Meggot was a Member of Parliament for that same borough. His mother was the granddaughter of Sir Gervase Elwes, 1st Baronet and Member of Parliament for Suffolk. Elwes inherited his first fortune from his father who died in 1718 when he was just four years old. Although his mother was left £100,000 in the will, she reputedly starved herself to death because she was too miserly to spend it. With her death, he inherited the family estate including Marcham Park at Marcham in Berkshire (now Oxfordshire).

Elwes the Miser.

The greatest influence on Elwes' life was his miserly uncle, Sir Harvey Elwes, 2nd Baronet of Stoke College and Member of Parliament for Sudbury, whom Elwes obsequiously imitated to gain favor. Sir Harvey prided himself on spending little more than £110 per annum. The two of them would spend the evening railing against other people's extravagances while they shared a single glass of wine. In 1751, in order to inherit his uncle's estate, he changed his name from Meggot to Elwes. Sir Harvey died on September 18, 1763, bequeathing his entire fortune to his nephew. The net worth of the estate was more than £250,000.

Elwes squandered more money on bad investments than he did on his living expenses. Still, today, Elwes would have been worth many millions. Despite his willingness to invest in business, Elwes became famous for his miserly ways in personal affairs. It was noted that he went to bed when darkness fell so as to save on candles. He began wearing only ragged clothes, and at one point he found a beggar's cast-off wig in a hedge and wore it for two weeks. His clothes were so dilapidated that many mistook him for a common street beggar and would put a penny into his hand as they passed. To avoid paying for a coach he would walk in the rain, and then sit in wet clothes to save the cost of a fire to dry them. His house was full of expensive furniture but also molding food. He would eat putrefied game before allowing new food to be bought. On one occasion it was said that he ate a moorhen that a rat had pulled from a river. Rather than spend the money for repairs he allowed his spacious country mansion to become uninhabitable. A near relative once stayed at his home in the country, but the bedroom was in such a poor state that the relative was kept awake all night by rain pouring on him from the roof. Unable to find a servant, the relative relocated his own bed several times himself until he found a place where no water leaked down upon him. Mentioning this to Elwes in the morning, the latter said, "Ay! I don't mind it myself . . . that is a nice corner in the rain!"

According to author William Haig Miller, Elwes even "complained bitterly of the birds robbing him of so much hay with which to build their nests." Even his health was limited by expense. In common with many misers he distrusted physicians, preferring to treat himself in order to save paying for one. He once badly cut both legs while walking home in the dark, but would only allow the apothecary to treat one, wagering his fee that the untreated limb would heal first. Elwes won by a fortnight and the doctor had to forfeit his fee. He also once bore a wound from a hunting accident. Legend has it that one day he was out shooting with a gentleman who was a particularly bad shot. This same man accidentally fired through a hedge, lodging several shot in the miser's cheek. With great embarrassment and concern, the gentleman approached Elwes to apologize. But Elwes, anticipating the apology, held out his hand and said, "My dear sir, I congratulate you on improving; I thought you would hit something in time."

In 1772 with the help of Lord Craven he became a Member of Parliament for Berkshire (his election expenses amounted to a mere eighteen pence). He entered the House of Commons in a by-election as a compromise candidate to replace Thomas Craven, which began the first of three terms. He held his seat unopposed until he stood down at the 1784 election. Elwes sat with either party according to his whim, and he never once rose to address the House of Commons. Fellow members mockingly observed that since he possessed only one suit, they could never accuse him of being a "turncoat." The post did, however, cause Elwes to frequently travel to London. This journey was accomplished on a poor, lean horse, the route chosen being always the one whereby he could avoid turnpike tolls. He was known to put a hard-boiled egg in his pocket, and midway on his journey would sit under some hedge and eat his egg or sleep. After twelve years he retired rather than face the prospect of laying out any money to retain his seat.

In the meantime, Elwes lost huge sums of money to his colleagues in unrepaid loans, uncollected debts, and dubious investments. Besides being a Member of Parliament, Elwes' accomplishments include financing the construction of a significant amount of Georgian London, including Portman Place, Portman Square, and parts of Oxford Circus Piccadilly, Baker Street, and Marylebone.

When his parliamentary career was over, Elwes devoted his full energies to being a miser as he moved about among his many properties. At his neglected estates he continued to forbid repairs, joined his tenants in postharvest gleaning, and sat with his servants in the kitchen to save the cost of a fire elsewhere. If a stableboy put out hay for a visitor's horse, Elwes would sneak out and remove it. In his last years he had no fixed abode and frequently stayed in his unrented London properties in the neighborhood of Marylebone. A couple of beds, a couple of chairs, a table, and an "old woman" (housekeeper) were said to be all his furnishings. This same housekeeper was known to frequently catch colds because there were never any fires and often no glass in the windows.

These practices nearly cost Elwes his life when he

fell desperately ill in one of his houses and no one could find him. Only by chance was he rescued. His nephew, Colonel Timms, inquired in vain at Elwes' banker's and at other places. A potboy recollected having seen an "old beggar" go into a stable at one of Elwes' uninhabited houses in Great Marlborough Street and lock the door behind him. Timms knocked at the door, but when no one answered he sent for a blacksmith and had the lock forced. In his book *Old and New London: Volume 4*, Edward Walford wrote, "In the lower part [of the house] all was shut and silent, but on ascending the stairs they heard the moans of a person seemingly in distress. They went to the chamber, and there on an old pallet bed they found Mr. Elwes, apparently in the agonies of death."

He remained in this condition until some "cordials" could be administered by a neighboring apothecary. After he had sufficiently recovered, Elwes stated that he believed he had been ill for "two or three days" and that there was an "old woman" in the house, but he supposed she had "gone away." Upon searching the premises, Timms and the apothecary found the woman stretched lifeless on the floor, having been dead for two days.

Toward the end of his life Elwes grew feverish and restless, hoarding small quantities of money in different places and continually visiting them to see that they were safe. He began suffering from delusion, fearing that he would die in poverty. In the night he was heard struggling with imaginary robbers. The family doctor was sent for, and looking at the dying miser was heard to remark, "That man, with his original strength of constitution, and life-long habits of temperance, might have lived twenty years longer but for his continual anxiety about money." Even his barrister, who drew up his £800,000 will, was forced to undertake his writings in the firelight by the dying man's bedside in order to save the cost of a candle.

The famed miser was also known to sleep in the same worn garments he wore during the day. He was discovered one morning between the sheets with his tattered shoes on his feet, an old torn hat on his head, and a stick in his hand. It was in this condition that he died on November 26, 1789. His burial took place in Stoke-by-Clare. After having lived on only £50 a year, Elwes left £500,000 to his two sons who were born out of wedlock, George and John (whom he loved but would not educate, believing that "putting things into people's heads is the sure way to take money out of their pockets"), and the rest to his nephew.

His friend and biographer, Edward Topham, remarked, ". . . his public character lives after him pure and without stain. In private life, he was chiefly an enemy to himself. To others, he lent much; to himself, he denied everything. But in the pursuit of his property, or in the recovery of it, I have it not in my remembrance one unkind thing that ever was done by him."

And Dickens himself may as well have been describing Elwes when he writes of Scrooge in Stave 2:

"I'm sure he is very rich, Fred," hinted Scrooge's niece. "At least you always tell me so."

"What of that, my dear!" said Scrooge's nephew. "His wealth is of no use to him. He don't do any good with it. He don't make himself comfortable with it. He hasn't the satisfaction of thinking—ha, ha, ha!—that he is ever going to benefit us with it."

Indeed, Scrooge inhabited a part of Dickens' own soul. As biographer Peter Ackroyd noted, "So it is perhaps only in fiction such as A Christmas Carol that his real preoccupation with money can come to the fore. Miserliness is a vice. Generosity is a virtue. How people obtain money. How people exert power over others because of money. How money can be an aspect of cruelty. How money can destroy a family. How the want of money is oppressive. How the greed for it is a form of unworthiness, a form of human alienation. And, central to A Christmas Carol, how the experiences of childhood can lead ineluctably to miserliness itself. For, if Scrooge is in one sense an exaggerated aspect of Dickens himself, it is clear that the author knew where the springs of at least his fictional character were buried—not only in the doomed childhood of the miser but also the anxiety which can emerge from it."

"He was halfway through a serialization that no one considered a success, and he was in conflict with his father and mother, as well as with his publishers," wrote Jane Smiley of Dickens at this juncture. "Just as every literary character is the author in some guise . . . so Ebenezer Scrooge was Charles Dickens, a man for whom money itself offered the prospect of safety, a man for whom isolation from the obligations of human relationship might be a form of peace."

In a sense, Dickens was struggling with himself and his past, and it would preoccupy him for the next six weeks until he wept and cried and laughed through the streets of London.

Dickens now had his miser. The venom would come later.

Scrooge and Marley

Scrooge never painted out Old Marley's name. There it stood, years afterwards, above the warehouse door: Scrooge and Marley. The firm was known as Scrooge and Marley.

While Charles Dickens never tells us precisely where Ebenezer Scrooge's counting house was located, the clues in A *Christmas Carol* suggest it was in the City of London. The "City" refers to a particular area of London, the core of roughly one square mile (it is even called "The Square Mile" colloquially) from which the capital historically grew. It was and continues to be the center of finance and commerce in London.

Indeed, today one can pass Simpson's, which has been serving mutton chops and roast beef to well-dressed City gentlemen since 1757.

"It was within this maze of alleyways that Dickens placed the counting house," wrote Richard Jones. "In this quaint, atmospheric backwater of twisting passage ways and dark courtyards, time appears to have stood still, and it is not difficult to conjure up images of Scrooge's neighbors 'wheezing up and down, heating their hands on their breasts, and stamping their feet upon the pavement stones to warm them.' "

We can guess this location partly because Scrooge is a trader, merchant, or businessman of some sort, but also because Dickens mentions several parts of the City by name. St Paul's Cathedral, with its famous dome, is mentioned in Stave I. And on his way home to Camden Town, Bob Cratchit (we only know him as Scrooge's anonymous clerk at this stage) slides down Cornhill (a City street) on the ice. As Camden Town is several miles northwest of the City, Scrooge's offices would certainly be somewhere east or south of Cornhill.

Describing the immediate vicinity of the office, Dickens mentions a courtyard and "the ancient tower of a church, whose gruff old bell was always peeping slyly down at Scrooge out of a Gothic window in the wall." The church may well be St Michael's, Cornhill, on which basis the City of London's Dickens Walk identifies the exact site of Scrooge & Marley's as Newman's Court.

Newman's Court is off the north side of Cornhill about 165 yards east of Bank Station and just east of Finch Lane. Located in the financial heart of the city, opposite the towering spire of St Michael's, Cornhill is the little covered alley where a Mr. Newman and his family set up home in 1650 amidst a bustling market. In the many changes that Cornhill has seen over the centuries and in this heyday of modern development when concrete frames filled with plate glass are shooting forever skyward, it is amazing how this Court and numerous others have survived. Old Newman would hardly recognize it now, with cars of Midland Bank employees parked where his house once stood. But, along with his descendants, he would probably be overjoyed to find it still here at all.

Newman's Court first became famous in 1652 when the first public coffeehouse in London opened there. A merchant by the name of Edwards, who traded in Turkey, brought with him some bags of coffee from the Levant, and a Greek servant knew how to prepare the blend. The new elixir was an instant success with Edwards' friends. The Greek servant, Pasquet (some have it as Pasqua), then opened the first public coffee house in London. It was an instant success.

Once upon a time—of all the good days in the year,
on Christmas Eve—old Scrooge sat busy in his counting-
house. It was cold, bleak, biting weather . . . .

A counting house, or compting house, literally is the building, room, office, or suite in which a business firm carries on operations, particularly accounting. By a synecdoche, it has come to mean the accounting operations of a firm, however housed. The term is British in origin and is primarily used in the context of the nineteenth century or earlier periods. Counting house is also the name given to early businesses which safely stored public and private money and loaned money.

By today's standard definitions, a counting house would be called an accountant's office. In Victorian England, these offices handled financial transactions for clients, such as collecting rent, paying bills, auditing etc. It also probably served the function of being a loan office or a collection office. Clerks and executives would literally be counting money in the "counting house." Then they would fill out the ledgers of their clients and harbor the money collected. Such offices would be filled with numerous ledgers, which required constant copying, and large and small cash boxes with which to keep the money safe.

It has been pointed out by literary historian Ruth Richardson that Dickens might have gotten the name for the firm of Scrooge and Marley from a sign from a neighborhood where he lived in his late teens. Richardson pointed out that Dickens' address at this time had changed over the years, and that the east Marleybone Street address had become 22 Cleveland Street, and before that it was 10 Norfolk Street. She further revealed that in the same neighborhood at the same time there was a sculptor who was derided by locals as a miser, and also that there was a sign nearby with the name "Goodge and Marney" signaling the workplace of two tradesmen, and finally a local cheesemonger by the name of "Marley." There is little question that these names probably figured into Dickens' process of creating the enigmatic sign hanging above old Scrooge's office. It seems that, in addition to the reference above, the name "Marley" showed up in a lot of places where Dickens might have poached it from.

Fred

"A merry Christmas, uncle! God save you!" cried a cheerful voice. It was the voice of Scrooge's nephew, who came upon him so quickly that this was the first intimation he had of his approach.

"Bah!" said Scrooge, "Humbug!"

He had so heated himself with rapid walking in the fog and frost, this nephew of Scrooge's, that he was all in a glow; his face was ruddy and handsome; his eyes sparkled, and his breath smoked again.

Scrooge's nephew Fred is a jovial, well-intentioned man. But who is Fred?

There is no question among scholars that Fred was probably based on Fredrick Dickens, Charles' brother of his youth. Fred had been born on July 4, 1820. Fred attended a school in Hampstead with their brother Alfred Dickens for two years, until their father John Dickens could no longer afford the fees. At the end of the school day, the boys would be collected by their older brother, Charles.

When John Dickens was imprisoned for debt on February 20, 1824, in the Marshalsea Debtors' Prison, Elizabeth Barrow Dickens and her three youngest children, including 4-year-old Fred, joined her husband there in April of that year.

In 1834, at the age of fourteen, Charles took Fred in when he moved into a three-room apartment in Furnival's Inn. By then, the word was out that Dickens was in fact Boz, the writer of *The Pickwick Papers*. He was still a reporter and was making £275 a year, a very nice sum in those days for a young man on the rise. Charles was now twenty-two years old, and he was slowly becoming the man of the family.

His father had continued to struggle. In the intervening years, Charles, already an established court reporter, had helped find jobs for his father who lost many of them. And Charles' own finances became worse and worse; at one point, he spent every penny he had to keep his father from debtors' prison once again, only to find that there were other creditors unknown to the family who were ready to press new charges.

In an effort to change the fortunes of his mother and father, Charles arranged for new and less-expensive lodgings for them and his remaining young siblings. And in an effort to help his young brother, Fred, of whom he was very fond, he took him in.

"Furnival's Inn was inhabited largely by solicitors with comfortable incomes. The rent of 35 pounds a year that Dickens paid was not small, and he himself would have been in no difficulties but for his father's debts," wrote Edgar Johnson.

American journalist Nathaniel Parker Willis, who visited the young writer at his home, remarked on the Spartan accommodations after climbing three flights of stairs and coming "into an uncarpeted and bleak-looking room, with a deal table, two or three chairs and a few books, a small boy, and Mr. Dickens for all the contents."

Fred and Charles spent much time together. Dickens worked furiously during the day as a reporter, then came home nights to work on *Sketches by Boz*. Fred was always a help. In fact, when Dickens' future wife, Catherine Hogarth, took ill with a cold, Charles dispatched Fred to Catherine with a jar of blackcurrant jam. Dickens took great interest in his younger brother, almost paternal, and his fiancé was fond of Fred as well. Fred proved himself dependable, and most importantly loyal, to Charles. They had become very close. And it was Charles' wish that he school Fred so that Fred would not end up unable to manage his own finances like their father, but to be a solvent and reliable man.

And of course it was Dickens who helped Fred, at fifteen years old, find his first job. Writing to his friend Macrone, "I have deliberated a long time about the propriety of keeping him at his present study, but I am convinced that at his present period of life, it is really only so much a waste of time." Dickens insisted that Fred take tea at home so that he might continue studying; he thought it a good idea for Fred to take a stool and learn good business habits. Dickens said of Fred to Macrone that "any sharp young fellow, you could not have better suited to your purposes."

After Charles married Kate, Fred continued to live with Charles in new lodgings at Doughty Street. "The Doughty Street home was soon full of lively doings. In addition to Mary, young Fredrick Dickens—by this time sixteen—was now a member of the household, and added to its high spirits. A full-lipped, snub-nosed youth, with raised eyebrows and an amusing oily laugh, he had a ludicrous gift for comic imitations in which Dickens abetted him. The bright, first-floor sitting room often resounded with Kate's and Mary's happy laughter."

And when Kate's sister Mary was suddenly seized by a grave illness, of whom Charles was immensely fond, shortly thereafter it was Fred who, in the middle of the night, ran through the streets of London to fetch the doctor to no avail.

By now Fred was growing into a gentleman, and Dickens succeeding in getting Lord Stanley to appoint his brother to the Secretary's Office in the Custom House. The two remained close, and when Dickens took a small summer home in Broadstairs, Fred came to visit. He was a popular personality in the house with friends and family alike. Fred and Mitton would trade barbs and laughs for long periods of time. And Fred and Charles would go aboard ships, keeping the sailors laughing by roaring out a series of completely absurd nautical commands in full loud burst with all the seriousness they could muster, generally keeping the crews in stitches.

It was not uncommon for Fred, the most popular of uncles with Charles and Kate's brood, to care for the children in the couple's absence. And when Dickens and Kate traveled to America the first time in 1842, the 22-year-old Fred was left in charge of their young family. As Dickens once wrote to a friend, he trusted Fred so much that he even entrusted him with the key to their wine cellar.

Dickens wrote to Forster before their trip to America that Kate "is satisfied to have nobody in the house but Fred, of whom, as you know, they are all fond. He has got his promotion, and they give him the increased salary from the day on which the minute was made by Baring, I feel so amiable, so meek, so fond of people, so full of gratitudes and reliances, that I am like a sick man.

And I am already counting the days between this and coming home again."

But by 1843 something between Dickens and Fred had started to go wrong. His father's continued irresponsibility and the careers of his brothers worried him greatly. According to Johnson, "Fred, although his Treasury salary had been increased, was falling into his father's extravagant ways." A creditor at Gray's Inn sent Dickens "for the second time a bill which I think is Frederick's." Dickens told Mitton (friend to both) that Fred seemed to resent the way that Dickens had resolved the matter. Fred responded by staying away from Devonshire Terrace, now the abode of the large Dickens family.

Devonshire Terrace was a large home fit for a London gentleman. In it Dickens had installed "mahogany doors, bookshelves, mantelpieces, great mirrors on the walls, thick carpets, white print roller-blinds at every window, and the best available bathroom fittings. A dining room table with five additional leaves was especially made for the columned dining room, and twelve leather chairs. The library became his study, its French windows opening on to a flight of steps down into the garden. There were nurseries in the attics, kitchens in the basement, cellars, a butler's pantry and a coach house. . . ." wrote biographer Claire Tomalin.

"Your absence from here," Dickens wrote to Fred, "had been your own act always. I shall be perfectly glad to see you; and should have been, at any time."

And it is at this stage in the relationship with Charles and Fred, that Scrooge meets his nephew Fred. In this scene, Charles plays out his anger with his brother for his spendthrift ways, as he veers ever closer to their father's extravagance:

> *What's Christmas time to you but a time for paying bills without money; a time for finding yourself a year older, but not an hour richer; a time for balancing your books and having every item in 'em through a round dozen of months presented dead against you?*

One cannot help but hear the brother chastise the brother and father in this condemnation from Charles. Given Fred and Charles' childhood, this fear of indebtedness, prison, poverty, and the inability to manage one's business affairs was like a mark on the family that Charles was so sad to see in his brother's personality.

To be sure, Dickens' condemnation was severe. Charles himself had faced debt and borrowed money to get out of it all his life. But to see his brother fall victim to this particular demon was a difficult pill for Charles to swallow.

More bitter still was Fred's sudden absence. Fred was as big a personality as Charles in their home. He was well loved by the family. The laughter he caused through his jokes and general buffoonery had left the house quieter in his absence than it had been. Dickens and Kate missed that.

For his part, Dickens put his most heartfelt feelings in Fred's mouth, when in the story Fred says to Scrooge:

> "There are many things from which I might have derived good, by which I have not profited, I dare say," returned the nephew. "Christmas among the rest. But I am sure I have always thought of Christmas time, when it has come round—apart from the veneration due to its sacred name and origin, if anything belonging to it can be apart from that—as a good time; a kind, forgiving, chari-table, pleasant time; the only time I know of, in the long calendar of the year, when men and women seem by one consent to open their shut-up hearts freely, and to think of people below them as if they really were fellow-passengers to the grave, and not another race of creatures bound on other journeys. And therefore, uncle, though it has never put a scrap of gold or silver in my pocket, I believe that it has done me good, and will do me good; and I say, God bless it!"

The enmity between them vexed Dickens as he walked the streets. There is no question that there is a part of Charles in Scrooge, angry at his brother. But there is also a part of Charles that missed his well-natured brother:

"I want nothing from you; I ask nothing of you; why cannot we be friends?"

"Good afternoon," said Scrooge.

"I am sorry, with all my heart, to find you so resolute. We have never had any quarrel, to which I have been a party. But I have made the trial in homage to Christmas, and I'll keep my Christmas humor to the last. So a Merry Christmas, uncle!"

It was yet another worry that kept Dickens up at night, and a difficult and painful relationship to sift through as he walked the streets of London.

The Solicitors

"At this festive season of the year, Mr. Scrooge," said the gentleman, taking up a pen, "it is more than usually desirable that we should make some slight provision for the Poor and destitute, who suffer greatly at the present time. Many thousands are in want of common necessaries; hundreds of thousands are in want of common comforts, sir."

If John Elwes was a well-remembered but odd character, Robert Malthus provided the venom that Dickens put in Scrooge's mouth.

The Reverend Thomas Robert Malthus was born on February 13, 1766 and died on December 23, 1834. Malthus was an English cleric and influential scholar in the fields of political economy and demography.

And there is no question that Dickens used the fact of Malthus' death date, the day before Christmas Eve, as one similar in bearing to Marley.

"Mr. Marley has been dead these seven years," Scrooge replied. *"He died seven years ago, this very night."*

Malthus became widely known for his theories about change in population. His *An Essay on the Principle of Population* observed that sooner or later population will be checked by famine and disease, leading to what is known as a Malthusian Catastrophe. He wrote in opposition to the popular view in eighteenth-century Europe that saw society as improving and in principle as perfectible. He wrote of how the dangers of population growth precluded progress toward a utopian society:

"The power of population is indefinitely greater than the power in the earth to produce subsistence for man. . . . That the increase of population is necessarily limited by the means of subsistence, That population does invariably increase when the means of subsistence increase, and, That the superior power of population is repressed, and the actual population kept equal to the means of subsistence, by misery and vice."

Malthus placed the long-term stability of the economy above short-term expediency. He criticized the Poor Laws (which were set up to help the poor) and, alone among important contemporary economists, he supported the Corn Laws (which introduced a system of taxes on British imports of wheat to benefit wealthy landowners and artificially drive up the price of bread for all, making it all but unaffordable for the poor and working class).

"The power of population is so superior to the power of the earth to produce subsistence for man, that premature death must in some shape or other visit the human race. The vices of mankind are active and able ministers of depopulation," Malthus wrote in his 1789 book *An Essay on the Principle of Population*. "They are the precursors in the great army of destruction, and often finish the dreadful work themselves. But should they fail in this war of extermination, sickly seasons, epidemics, pestilence, and plague advance in terrific array, and sweep off their thousands and tens of thousands. Should success be still incomplete, gigantic inevitable famine stalks in the rear, and with one mighty blow levels the population with the food of the world."

Malthus' disciples perceived the ideas of charity toward the poor, typified by Tory paternalism, were futile, as these would only result in increased numbers of the poor. These ideas found vice in Whig economic ideas best exemplified by the Poor Law Amendment Act of 1834. The Act was described by opponents as "a Malthusian bill designed to force the poor to emigrate, to work for lower wages, to live on a coarser sort of food," and it initiated the construction of workhouses despite riots and arson.

Dickens was diametrically opposed, writing to his friend Forster years later, "I don't believe now they ever would have carried the repeal of the corn law, if they could," referring to Whigs and Tories alike. According to Forster, "he ascribed it to a secret belief 'in the gentle politico-economical principle that a surplus population must and ought to starve.' "

"The great Malthusian dread was that 'indiscriminate charity' would lead to exponential growth in the population in poverty, increased charges to the public purse to support this growing army of the dependent, and, eventually, the catastrophe of national bankruptcy," wrote Dr. Dan Ritschel, at the University of Maryland. "Though Malthusianism has since come to be identified with the issue of general over-population, the original Malthusian concern was more specifically with the fear of over-population by the dependent poor!"

It was clear at the time that the Industrial Revolution was taking hold in England. As it began to rise, some of the negative effects became obvious—growing urbanization begat rising unemployment and with that poverty increased; "Poor Laws" (first established in 1601) were an attempt to provide a safety net for those at the bottom of the economy.

But the laws were unpopular with many. The English propertied class denied responsibility for poverty and actively opposed what they viewed as income redistribution. In 1832 a Royal Commission published its findings, which had probably been predetermined, stating that the old system was badly and expensively run. In 1834 the Poor Law Amendment Act (PLAA) was an Act of the Parliament of the United Kingdom passed by the Whig government of Earl Grey that reformed the country's poverty-relief system. The PLAA curbed the cost of poor relief, which had been spiraling throughout the nineteenth century, and led to the creation of workhouses. Many who wrote and passed the laws were acolytes of Malthus.

"I wish to be left alone," said Scrooge. "Since you ask me what I wish, gentlemen, that is my answer. I don't make merry myself at Christmas and I can't afford to make idle people merry. I help to support the establishments I have mentioned—they cost enough; and those who are badly off must go there."

"Many can't go there; and many would rather die."

"If they would rather die," said Scrooge, "they had better do it, and decrease the surplus population."

In England and Wales a workhouse, colloquially known as a "spike," was a place where those unable to support themselves were offered accommodation and

employment. The earliest known use of the term dates
from 1631. Life in a workhouse was intended to be harsh,
to deter the able-bodied poor, and to ensure that only
the truly destitute would apply. But in areas such as the
provision of free medical care and education for children,
neither of which was available to the poor in England
living outside workhouses in Victorian times, workhouse
inmates were advantaged over the general population,
a dilemma that the Poor Law authorities never managed
to reconcile. As the nineteenth century wore on, workhouses increasingly became refuges for the elderly, infirm,
and sick rather than the able-bodied poor.

Victorian Workhouses were dreary places, and many
of the blueprints for these "state of the art" buildings
of the period were in fact the blueprint for the modern
prison today, with giant walls, a central tower, and long
three-story shed rows spiking out of the central tower.
They were actually referred to as "pauper bastilles."
The work in workhouses was menial at best, and few ever
really learned a trade. Many were asked to tend the sick
or teach, but many of those chosen did not have the skill
set to do either.

For instance, a breakfast of bread and gruel was
followed by a midday dinner that might consist of cooked
meats, pickled pork or bacon with vegetables, potatoes,
yeast dumplings, soup, suet, and rice pudding. Supper
was normally bread, cheese, and broth, and sometimes

butter or potatoes. The larger workhouses had separate dining rooms for males and females; workhouses without separate dining rooms would stagger the meal times to avoid any contact between the sexes.

But it was no coincidence that Malthus had died on December 23, 1834, eight years before *A Christmas Carol* was written, and only a year before Jacob Marley. There was no doubt in Victorian England whose voice had been imparted to Scrooge and Marley.

Bob Cratchit

The door of Scrooge's counting-house was open that he might keep his eye upon his clerk, who in a dismal little cell beyond, a sort of tank, was copying letters.

For inspiration in creating Bob Cratchit, Dickens did not have to walk very far. He strode out of his home at 1 Devonshire near Regent's Park and walked northward toward the dour neighborhood of Camden Town. It was not more than a three mile or so walk, a short brisk walk for Dickens in 1843. But he would return here now and again. Despite the poverty, crime, and everything else he saw late at night on his walks along various routes, nothing could have been more disturbing than to visit Camden Town.

It may be supposed that Camden Town, for Dickens, was filled with images of his youth that were still very hard indeed to deal with. It held certain stories in his life he would not offer up to anyone until he neared his death. The area, for Dickens, was charged with emotion. There was no question that Scrooge's mistreated clerk would live in Camden Town, which Dickens had passed on the train not so long ago on his way to Manchester.

And there was also no question that Cratchit would be the anvil that Scrooge would hammer down upon. Scrooge would mistreat the poor clerk, blow after unyielding blow, yet Bob Cratchit remained. For all mistreatment at Scrooge's hands, Cratchit would symbolize the best part of the working class in that day and age.

Bob Cratchit is surely one of the most sympathetic characters in all of Dickens' works, and it is surely ironic, then, that Bob Cratchit and the Cratchit family are based on John Dickens and his family through Charles' experiences as a child.

John Dickens was the son of William Dickens (1719–1785) and Elizabeth Ball (1745–1824). He was a clerk in the Royal Navy Pay Office at Portsmouth in Hampshire. He married Elizabeth Barrow in June 1803 in London. They had seven children. The Royal Navy moved Dickens around somewhat. He was transferred to London, and then to Chatham, returning to live in Camden Town in London in 1822 to work in Somerset House.

John Dickens.

Charles Dickens was the oldest boy born to John and Elizabeth. While they lived in Chatham, Charles enjoyed what he considered an idyllic childhood. He was happy in his schooling, they lived a comfortable life, and Dickens played with Fanny along with a number of their brothers and sisters. And he was quite content. His memories of Chatham were the fondest of his entire childhood.

Eventually, John Dickens was relocated, once again, back to London. The family moved into a tenement with eight people living in the house at 16 Bayham Street.

"I thought in the little back garret of Bayham Street of all that I had lost in losing Chatham," Dickens wrote years later of his depression at this time.

"Bayham Street was about the poorest part of the London suburbs then," recalled Forster, "and the house was a mean small tenement, with a wretched little back-garden abutting on a squalid court. Here was no place for new acquaintances to him: no boys were near with whom he might hope to become in any way familiar. A washerwoman lived next door, and a Bow-Street officer lived over the way. Many, many times has he spoken to me of this, and how he seemed at once to fall into a solitary condition apart from all other boys of his own age, and to sink into a neglected state at home which had been always quite unaccountable to him. . . . That he took, from the very beginning of this Bayham-Street life, his first impression of that struggling poverty which is nowhere more vividly shown than in the commoner streets of the ordinary London suburb."

Charles Dickens' boyhood home at 16 Bayham Street in Camden Town.

The neighborhood was marked by the St. Martin's almshouses, or poor houses, set up to help the aged and the unemployed. Founded in 1818 they stayed fixed in Dickens' memory for his lifetime.

"The housing was uninspiring, so it was no great loss when the railway cut through the area in the 1840s," wrote Daniel Tyler, a London historian. "Its tenements were demolished at the start of the twentieth century." The building at 16 Bayham Street exists no more, a victim of time and progress. But there are still three examples of these types of homes on that street surviving in the city to this day.

John Dickens was a clerk, and living in London was expensive. He found it difficult to provide for his growing family on his meager income. Soon his debts had become so severe that all the household goods were sold in an attempt to pay his bills, including furniture and silverware. Dickens' memories of those days were dark and gloomy.

Dickens himself later described the neighborhood in *Dombey and Son*, writing, "a little row of houses, with little squalid patches of ground before them, fenced off with old doors, barrel staves, scraps of tarpaulin, and dead bushes; with bottomless tin kettles and exhausted iron fenders, thrust into the gaps."

There is no question that Dickens, angry at his own father for the strife inflicted on his family through his spendthrift ways, still paints a sympathetic portrait of the man as working-class hero.

"Let me hear another sound from you," said Scrooge, "and you'll keep your Christmas by losing your situation! . . . There's another fellow," muttered Scrooge; who overheard him: "my clerk, with fifteen shillings a week, and

a wife and family, talking about a merry Christmas. I'll retire to Bedlam."

What Dickens was railing against in those days was his utter sense at the devaluation of human life during the roaring days of the Industrial Revolution in England at the time. England was at the mercy of the "economic man" who placed all value on things in what the market would bear. Services as well as goods were subject only to the laws of the free economy. There was no just or fair pricing for either goods or services. Buy low and sell high was the only rule. Workers in many cases were not treated with much more respect than things, and were instantly replaceable in this economy with a vast pool of hands waiting for the next worker to go down. And industrials liked this because it kept that waiting throng as cheap as the workers they hired. There were no protections. Especially in the days before unionization, workers had little leverage.

"To say . . . " wrote Edgar Johnson, "that Scrooge is paying Cratchit all he is worth on the open market (or he would get another job) is to take for granted the very conditions Dickens is attacking. It is not only that timid, uncompetitive people like Bob Cratchit may lack the courage to bargain for their own rights. But, as Dickens well knows, there are many things other than the man's work that determine his wage—the existence of a large body of other men able to do the same job. And if Cratchit is getting the established remuneration for his work, that makes the situation worse. . . . What Dickens has at heart is not any economic conception like Marx's labor theory of value, but a feeling of the human value of human beings."

"To be sure the Cratchits are fictional creations. But as social types, even though they are surely exaggerated, they are not altogether unreal," wrote Stephen Nissenbaum. Cratchit is not a working-class employee. The working class in Victorian Britain were industrial laborers. Cratchit was a clerk, a mid-level trained employee. As Nissenbaum argues, Cratchit was indeed a trusted employee, regardless of his treatment. "Cratchit is literate . . . and so at least is one of his sons."

> "A poor excuse for picking a man's pocket every twenty-fifth of December!" said Scrooge, buttoning his great-coat to the chin. "But I suppose you must have the whole day. Be here all the earlier next morning."
>
> The clerk promised that he would; and Scrooge walked out with a growl. The office was closed in a twinkling, and the clerk, with the long ends of his white comforter dangling below his waist (for he boasted no great-coat), went down a slide on Cornhill, at the end of a lane of boys, twenty times, in honor of its being Christmas Eve, and then ran home to Camden Town as hard as he could pelt, to play at blindman's-buff."

Bob Cratchit walked to work, and he went by the route that took him through Cornhill Road. Like Dickens himself, there was a large portion of the society that walked great distances every day. Cratchit was typical of his age in this way. He walked three or more miles every day from Bayham Street all the way to Newman's Court.

"Most people walked to and from work. The first commuters were walkers and the distances they covered were long by modern standards. As London grew in the opening years of the nineteenth century, so the distances between home and work increased. In A Christmas Carol Bob Cratchit seems to think nothing of walking from Camden Town to Scrooge's counting house off Cornhill in the city," wrote Dickens scholar Andrew Sanders. "These tended to be lower-middle-class Londoners. Bob Cratchit in A Christmas Carol daily retraces much of the boy Dickens' route into central London from his house in Camden Town."

"Cities fostered new breeds of walkers. The disciplined pedestrian, the speeding commuter, the idylling window shopper," and many others walked long distances, wrote Anthony Amato in A History of Walking. Historian Paul Langford notes the existence of what one editor of Traveler's Tales called "a craving for locomotion" and another commentator described as "a perfect mania the English have for moving about from one place to another." According to Langford the need of the restless English to be up and about—"jaunting around" to use a phrase from the period—made them Europe's first commuters.

Like Bob Cratchit, John Dickens was one such commuter, walking three to four miles each way to work each day from 16 Bayham Street to Somerset House on the south side of the Strand in central London, over-looking the River Thames, just east of Waterloo Bridge.

Despite all his failings as a provider and role model, or later as a troublesome dependent, Dickens wrote lovingly of his father years later. "I know my father to be as kind-hearted and generous a man as ever lived in the world. Everything that I can remember of his conduct to his wife, or children, or friends, in sickness or affliction, is beyond all praise. By me, as a sick child, he has watched night and day, unweariedly and patiently, many nights and days. He never undertook any business, charge, or trust that he did not zealously, conscientiously, punctually, honorably discharge."

Jacob Marley

Marley was dead: to begin with. There is no doubt whatever about that. The register of his burial was signed by the clergyman, the clerk, the undertaker, and the chief mourner. Scrooge signed it. And Scrooge's name was good upon 'Change, for anything he chose to put his hand to. Old Marley was as dead as a door-nail.

This fanciful beginning was grabbed by Dickens from a dream he had had the summer just past. While visiting Broadstairs, where he had had the dream of the skewered baby. As Dickens described it, "a private gentleman and a particular friend" was pronounced, "as dead Sir . . . as a door nail." The dream had stuck with him, and shaken him at the time. It was still so severe upon him that he expunged it, in a way, by using it to start the book.

According to Dickens, "Scrooge and he were partners for I don't know how many years. Scrooge was his sole executor, his sole administrator, his sole assign, his sole legatee, his sole friend, and sole mourner." Robert Malthus died on December 24, 1836. But who was Marley and where did he come from?

In addition to Richardson's contribution to understanding the origin of Marley's name—based on Dickens' time near east Marleybone street—there are still other theories. It has been suggested that Jacob Marley was named for Marley Tunnel, a small tunnel on the railway line from Exeter to Plymouth. Once again, the newly expanding British railways may have played a hand in the formation of A Christmas Carol. The Exeter to Plymouth line, also called the South Devon Main Line, is a central part of the trunk railway line between London Paddington and Penzance in the southern United Kingdom. It is a major branch of the Great Western Main Line and runs from Exeter, to Plymouth, from where it continues as the Cornish Main Line. In 1948 it became part of the Western Region of British Railways and is now part of the Network Rail system.

The steep climb up Rattery Bank starts right from the end of the platform, a stiff challenge in those days to trains that called at Totnes. At the top is Rattery Viaduct and the 869-yard-long Marley Tunnel. The original single-track tunnel had a second bore added alongside it in 1893 when the line was doubled. The line today runs along the southern edge of Dartmoor.

Dickens often found names while traveling, much like he did Ebenezer Scrooge's name. However, Marley's first name, Jacob, has a different history. In fact it is not known whether Dickens chose the name with a purpose or not. The biblical story of Jacob is told in the Book of Genesis. The story "Jacob's Ladder" is named after his vision of a ladder that climbs to heaven and provides escape for the Israelites. After being estranged from his mother, father, and brother, Jacob returned to his homeland seeking reconciliation, especially with his brother, Esau. He was alone at the time, hoping to find peace with God the night before their family's reunion. That night, in the dark, he wrestled with what he thought was a man until the break of day. As the light of dawn broke, and Jacob could see the shadow he'd been wrestling with all night, Jacob insisted that the man bestow a blessing on him. The "man" revealed himself to be an angel of God. The angel then blessed Jacob and gave him the name "Israel" (Yisrael), meaning "the one who wrestled with God."

Is it a coincidence that Jacob Marley, who comes to visit Scrooge in the dark black hours of the night, is himself struggling with God and his own deeds? Though Dickens struggled with organized religion, he was probably well acquainted with Genesis and Jacob.

At the very least, it proves to be an interesting coincidence.

Certainly among the most visual scenes in "Stave 1: Marley's Ghost" is when Scrooge comes to the threshold of his lodgings and sees Marley's face in the doorknocker. It must be remembered that the house where Scrooge lives was previously Marley's home, and that Scrooge had inherited it upon Marley's death.

The yard was so dark that even Scrooge, who knew its every stone, was fain to grope with his hands. The fog and frost so hung about the black old gateway of the house, that it seemed as if the Genius of the Weather sat in mournful meditation on the threshold.

Now, it is a fact, that there was nothing at all particular about the knocker on the door, except that it was very large. It is also a fact, that Scrooge had seen it, night and morning, during his whole residence in that place; also that Scrooge had as little of what is called fancy about him as any man in the city of London, even including—which is a bold word—the corporation, aldermen, and livery. Let it also be borne in mind that Scrooge had not bestowed one thought on Marley, since his last mention of his seven years' dead partner that afternoon. And then let any man explain to me, if he can, how it happened that Scrooge, having his key in the lock of the door, saw in the knocker, without its undergoing any intermediate process of change—not a knocker, but Marley's face.

Marley's face. It was not in impenetrable shadow as the other objects in the yard were, but had a dismal light about it, like a bad lobster in a dark cellar. It was not angry or ferocious, but looked at Scrooge as Marley used to look: with ghostly spectacles turned up on its ghostly forehead. The hair was curiously stirred, as if by breath or hot air; and, though the eyes were wide open, they were perfectly motionless. That, and its livid color, made it horrible; but its horror seemed to be in spite of the face and beyond its control, rather than a part of its own expression.

As Scrooge looked fixedly at this phenomenon, it was a knocker again.

Where does this scene come from? It goes back to the walks Dickens himself made night after night, especially during the writing of A Christmas Carol, as his writing powers, self-admittedly, were never greater upon him.

The illustration of Marley's Ghost by John Leech

in the first edition of A Christmas Carol.

"Dickens's walks served him in two ways. On one level, they were fact-finding missions during which he recorded with his keen eye the teeming urban landscapes whose descriptions were his stock-in-trade," wrote Merrell Noden in *Sports Illustrated*. In a letter to a friend, while visiting Paris years later, Dickens admitted to walking the streets, "wandering into Hospitals, Prisons, Dead-houses, Operas, Theatres, Concert-rooms, Burial-grounds, Palaces and Wine Shops. In my unoccupied fortnight of each month, every description of gaudy and ghastly sight has been passing before me in rapid Panorama."

"But Dickens's walks played another, more important role in his life. They were, in a sense, acts of self-preservation," reasoned Noden.

"If I could not walk far and fast," Dickens once confessed, "I think I should just explode and perish."

Dickens absolutely walked through the neighborhoods near where Charing Cross Station is today. One of the streets around there is Craven Street. The street is lined on both sides with red-brick eighteenth century townhouses. The address 40 Craven Street was the home of Dr. Charles West, founder of the Hospital for Sick Children.

West and Dickens had a common interest in the welfare of London's children. Dr. Charles West was an expert on diseases affecting women and children. He trained in medicine at Paris and Bonn where hospitals exclusively for children had long been in existence. Having returned to London in the early 1840s, West worked at the Universal Dispensary for Children and Women in Waterloo Road. He was determined to set up England's first inpatient hospital for children, but failed to persuade the managers of the dispensary to support his plan.

Through his own efforts, and through social contacts made by his fellow doctor, Henry Bence-Jones, a committee was formed in 1850 with support from eminent philanthropists and public-health reformers such as Lord Shaftesbury, Baroness Burdett-Coutts (a close friend of Dickens), and Edwin Chadwick of the Board of Health.

Indeed, later in life Dickens and West became very well acquainted. When West opened his hospital eight years after Dickens purloined one of the residences on West's street for A Christmas Carol, Dickens wrote a powerful article in his popular magazine Household Words to publicize it. Dickens and other eminent personalities of the time, including Oscar Wilde, senior clergymen of London, and members of the Royal Family, spoke at fundraisers such as the Annual Festival Dinner. In 1858 the Hospital survived its first major financial crisis after Dickens gave a public reading in aid of the hospital at St. Martin-in-the-Fields church hall. This raised enough money to enable the purchase of the neighboring house, 48 Great Ormond Street, increasing the bed capacity from 20 to 75.

But before that, perhaps in the fall of 1843, during one of his walks Dickens spied something unusual on Craven Street. "Legend holds that it was a grotesque old door knocker on one of the adjoining houses that gave Dickens the idea for Scrooge's door knocker turning into Marley's face in A Christmas Carol," wrote well-known

London tour guide Richard Jones. "Unfortunately, when an enthusiastic photographer approached the owner for permission to photograph the knocker, she is said to have removed it and placed it in a bank vault for safe keeping. Its whereabouts are now unknown."

Edgar Johnson wrote, "It should not be imagined that Christmas has for Dickens more than the very smallest connection with Christian dogma or theology. For Dickens Christmas is primarily a human not a super-natural feast. . . ." But even Johnson admits that "Marley's ghost is the symbol of divine grace, and that the three Christmas Spirits are the working of that grace through the agencies of memory, example, and fear."

There is also some question as to whether Marley's coming might have been inspired by some of the text from the Book of Revelation.

The lines "Behold, I stand at the door and knock. If anyone hears my voice and opens the door, then I will come in to him . . ." come from Revelations (3:20). And the message that Marley bears also comes from Revelation (3:17), where John writes to the Laodiceans, one of the seven major churches of Asia and a major center of wealth in those days, "Because thou say, 'I am rich, and increased with goods, and have need of nothing;' and knowest not that thou are the wretched, and miserable, and poor, and blind, and naked; I counsel thee to buy from me gold tried in the fire, that thou mayest be rich;

and white raiment, that thou mayest be clothed, and that the shame of thy nakedness do not appear; and anoint thine eyes with eye salve, that thou mayest see. . . ."

Again, in Dickens' era, familiarity with the Bible, especially among the middle and upper-middle class, was not to be expected. Indeed, the entire visit is presaged by the scene at the fireplace:

> *The fireplace was an old one, built by some Dutch merchant long ago, and paved all round with quaint Dutch tiles, designed to illustrate the Scriptures. There were Cains and Abels, Pharaoh's daughters, Queens of Sheba, Angelic messengers descending through the air on clouds like feather-beds, Abrahams, Belshazzars, Apostles putting off to sea in butter-boats, hundreds of figures to attract his thoughts; and yet that face of Marley, seven years dead, came like the ancient Prophet's rod, and swallowed up the whole. If each smooth tile had been a blank at first, with power to shape some picture on its surface from the disjointed fragments of his thoughts, there would have been a copy of old Marley's head on every one.*

The Bible stories and symbolism lent themselves nicely to the tale, but the fireplace had come from Dickens' past. While still in what he remembered as his idyllic childhood in Chatham, John Dickens' fortunes were already going downhill. In 1821 he was already spending too much money, and so they traded in their house on Ordnance Terrace to live at 18 St. Mary's Place, called "The Brook." This was the home where Charles and Fanny had looked out over a graveyard next to a church.

"There was a marked difference between Ordnance Terrace and the cramped cottage close to the parish church and the dockyard entrance. It stood in a mean thoroughfare called The Brook, which only twenty years before had been desirable; but the stream which ran down the lane had become a ditch of sewage, dependent on the rain to flush it, and The Brook was now full of taverns the Bell, the Golden Lion, the Three Cups, and the King's Head—beer-shops and lodging houses," explained Norman and Jeanne MacKenzie.

Dickens' upbringing was not particularly religious. But in the time they lived at St. Mary's Place, they may have spent more time in the church next door and they certainly befriended the Reverend Giles and his son. Still, Charles' memory of early religious training was rarely positive, as most boys of that age would agree. But for all his schooling, the most telling memory he had of religion came from the family fireplace in the house on St. Mary's Place whose tiles were illustrated with scenes from the scriptures, just like Scrooge's own fireplace! So Scrooge's fireplace comes from Dickens' childhood.

Dickens, like Twain later, found sitting through church services excruciating. He remembered being "dragged by the hair of my head" to listen to the preacher's sermons. And despite his best efforts to resist church and its teachings, it seemed the fireplace, and its stories, stuck with him. As biographer Peter Ackroyd jokingly remarked, "[H]e gave it to Scrooge, perhaps in revenge. . . ."

It is clear that some moral and biblical reckoning is at hand, if not just for Scrooge, for all of us. That Marley is shackled is part of that message.

> *The chain he drew was clasped about his middle. It was long, and wound about him like a tail; and it was made (for Scrooge observed it closely) of cashboxes, keys, padlocks, ledgers, deeds, and heavy purses wrought in steel. His body was transparent; so that Scrooge, observing him, and looking through his waistcoat, could see the two buttons on his coat behind.*
>
> *Scrooge had often heard it said that Marley had no bowels, but he had never believed it until now.*

When his father was a clerk in the Royal Navy pay yard in Chatham, Dickens would often take river trips and would have seen large chains and padlocks and cashboxes. And as Dickens was a former court reporter and visitor to the stock exchange, the cashboxes of the day were not unknown to him either. But it is no mistake that Dickens is painting what are the hard-won trophies of business as the sins of the middle and upper-middle merchant class. Again, it's a message that appears in Revelations.

When Marley's Ghost leaves and joins the countless other ghosts (some of whom Scrooge had also known in life) spiraling through London, he hovers near a homeless mother and child, unable to help. This is also part of the admonishment.

The visitation of Marley's Ghost is notice given, a sort of moral (if not religious) reckoning. Marley's spirit embodied Dickens' philosophies. Marley is Dickens' loud-speaker to the masses. "All through the Christian ages, and especially since the French Revolution, the Western world has been haunted by the idea of freedom and equality; it is only an idea, but it has penetrated to all ranks of society," wrote George Orwell about Dickens. "The most atrocious injustices, cruelties, lies, snobberies exist everywhere, but there are not many people who can regard these things with the same indifference as, say, a Roman slave-owner. Even the millionaire suffers from a vague sense of guilt, like a dog eating a stolen leg of mutton. Nearly everyone, whatever his actual conduct may be, responds emotionally to the idea of human brotherhood. Dickens voiced a code which was and on the whole still is believed in, even by people who violate it. It is difficult otherwise to explain why he could be both read by working people (a thing that has happened to no other novelist of his stature) and buried in Westminster Abbey."

Stave II

The Ghost
of Christmas Past

"Who, and what are you?" Scrooge demanded.

"I am the Ghost of Christmas Past."

"Long Past?" inquired Scrooge: observant of its dwarfish stature.

"No. Your past."

ickens scribbled away at his desk. . . .

Literary historian Mason Currey wrote about Dickens' writing desk, "His study had to be precisely arranged, with his writing desk placed in front of a window and, on the desk itself, his writing materials—goose quill pens and blue ink—laid out alongside several ornaments: a small vase of fresh flowers, a large paper knife, a gilt leaf with a rabbit perched upon it, and two bronze statuettes, one depicting a pair of fat toads dueling, the other a gentleman swarmed with puppies."

Charles Dickens at his writing desk.

Dickens was now writing in earnest. And though alternating between *Chuzzlewit* and *Carol* was difficult, Dickens put his mind to it. He had much work to do to in order to reveal the compelling past of his main character, and he set about doing so in his typical manner. According to his son Charles, "No city clerk was ever more methodical or orderly than he; no humdrum, monotonous, conventional task could ever have been discharged with more punctuality or with more business like regularity, than he gave to the work of his imagination and fancy."

Dickens was a worker. He was out of bed by 7 a.m. most mornings, and was at breakfast an hour later. He arrived at his study by 9 a.m. He needed peace and quiet in his study while he tried to write, going so far as having a second door to his study installed in one house so he could get it with a multitude of children, his wife, and her sister milling about. At 2 p.m. Dickens would emerge from his study and lunch with his family. Some days he chatted, others he chomped on his food, spoke barely a word, and raced back to his desk.

"On an ordinary day, he would complete about two-thousand words in this way, but during a flight of imagination he sometimes managed twice that amount," wrote Currey. "Other days, however, he would hardly write anything; nevertheless, he stuck to his work hours without fail, doodling and staring out the window to pass the time."

Sometimes he returned promptly to his study, some-times not. But he always ended his days with a brisk walk. It was his custom to continue to re-examine the stories he was working on, as he himself described it, "searching for some pictures I wanted to build upon." His brother-in-law remarked on Dickens returning from these walks, "he looked the personification of energy, which seemed to ooze from every pore as from some hidden reservoir."

Dickens could begin to see the book. And for it, he would want illustrations. By now it was near the third week of writing, and it was time to engage an illustrator. Hablot Knight Browne, also known as "Phiz," had been illustrating Dickens since *The Pickwick Papers*, and was engaged in illustrating *Martin Chuzzlewit*. Dickens decided to offer the opportunity to John Leech. Leech and Dickens had met years earlier when Dickens was interviewing illustrators for *The Pickwick Papers*. They had been introduced by a mutual friend, the famous caricaturist George Cruikshank. Leech had submitted his drawings and Dickens said some very favorable things about them. Leech mistakenly understood that the commission was his, and invited a friend out to dinner to celebrate. He was disappointed when he did not get the commission. But since the misunderstanding, Leech had blossomed into one of the most highly rated cartoonists of his day, no mean feat in the pen-and-ink days of the Victorian era.

Dickens was not dissatisfied with Browne, in fact it was quite the opposite. He was committed to Browne. However, Leech was persistent. Leech had once again submitted his name for the illustrating of *Martin Chuzzlewit* when its publication had been announced. But Dickens stuck with Browne for *Chuzzlewit*. Dickens wrote to Leech in 1842: "I have never forgotten having seen you some years ago, or ceased to watch your progress with much

THE GHOST OF CHRISTMAS PAST

interest and satisfaction. I congratulate you heartily on your success; and myself on having had my eye upon the means by which you have obtained it."

According to literary historian Michael Patrick Hearn, "The scheme of A Christmas Carol resembles that of another book illustrated by Leech, The Wassail Bowl (1842), a small volume bound in russet cloth with a Christmas device stamped in gold on the cover and illustrated with inserted teal etchings and textual wood-engravings. Dickens owned a copy of this book by his friend Albert Smith, and it may have influenced his decision to hire Leech for A Christmas Carol."

Now, with A Christmas Carol, Leech and Dickens could finally join forces. By the third week of October, Dickens had some material for Leech to examine. Dickens was paying for the illustrations himself on this printing, and decided on four wood engravings and four color plates to decorate the book.

"As with every other aspect of the design, Dickens went over each preliminary sketch with Leech," wrote literary historian Michael Patrick Hearn. "This was before the photographic age, so Leech had to draw each picture directly on the wood block to be engraved by William James Litton. Leech etched the four full-page plates himself, two to a steel plate as was the fashion at the time. He also made color sketches to guide the hand colorers."

John Leech's illustration of the Ghost of Christmas Past.

Dickens by now had wandered London far and wide, thinking through his plot. And now, with the stage set, and a sense of where he was going, he had to act out the transformation of his covetous old sinner Ebenezer Scrooge. It was somewhat easier said than done. But in the end, the three ghosts that were coming were nothing more than self-revelatory reexamination by none other than Dickens himself. And yet, it would be a trick to turn it regardless. An assessment of Scrooge's past would be necessary to begin turning that trick.

The School

"Good Heaven!" said Scrooge, clasping his hands together, as he looked about him. "I was bred in this place. I was a boy here!" . . .

"You recollect the way?" inquired the Spirit.

"Remember it!" cried Scrooge with fervor; "I could walk it blindfold."

The first ghost compelled a revisiting of his childhood and of his schooling. Now Dickens thought back on his own schoolboy teacher whom he had just seen while visiting Fanny in Manchester. As Dickens paced the streets of London, he traveled back in reverie to his childhood with his beloved teacher, William Giles, in the years before the Dickenses moved from Chatham to London.

"I was taken to Chatham when I was very young, and lived and was educated there till I was twelve or thirteen, I suppose," Dickens wrote to Mr. Wilkie Collins on June 6, 1865.

Giles' father, Rev. William Giles, was the minster at the Baptist Chapel nearest the school.

"It [the school] was very gravely and decorously ordered, and on a sound system; with an appeal on everything, to the honor and good faith of the boys, and an avowed intention to rely on their possession of those qualities, unless they proved themselves unworthy of it, which worked wonders," wrote Charles Dickens in *David Copperfield*.

The school consisted of several of Giles' younger siblings including John and Samuel, some children of the soldiers of the local garrison, and a few children of the neighbors. From all accounts Giles seems to have been taken with Dickens during Charles' stay there.

Charles Dickens' schoolboy teacher, William Giles.

According to biographer Robert Langton, Giles gave him "every encouragement in his power, even to making a companion of him of an evening, he was soon rewarded by the marked improvement that followed. Charles made rapid progress, and there is no doubt whatever that his wonderful knowledge and felicitous use of the English language in after life was, in great measure, due to the careful training of Mr. Giles, who was widely known as a cultivated reader and elocutionist."

All these boys were in great spirits, and shouted to each other, until the broad fields were so full of merry music, that the crisp air laughed to hear it!

"These are but shadows of the things that have been," *said the Ghost. "They have no consciousness of us."*

The jocund travellers came on; and as they came, Scrooge knew and named them every one. Why was he rejoiced beyond all bounds to see them! Why did his cold eye glisten, and his heart leap up as they went past!

Mrs. Godfrey, an older sister of one of Charles' schoolmates and a sister of Mr. Giles, remembered many years later, "Charles was quite at home at all sorts of parties, junkettings, and birthday celebrations, and that he took great delight in Fifth of November festivities around the bonfire."

Students at Mr. Giles' school were required to wear white beaver hats during their time there, and Dickens wore one until he left Chatham. Mary Weller, another student of the day, remembered that "they were not always learning, they had the merriest games that they ever played. They rowed up the river in the summer, and skated upon the ice in the winter. They had holidays too, and Twelfth cakes, and parties, when they danced till midnight. As to friends, they had such dear friends, and so many of them, that I want time to reckon them up. They were all young, like the handsome boy."

He wrote a story called "Misnar, The Sultan of India!" and was well-liked for storytelling and entertaining his classmates. Charles was also a voracious reader, and ate up volumes by Defoe, Goldsmith, and Fielding.

"The school room setting adds, moreover, a layer of irony, conscious or unconscious, because it was a school that the boy in the blacking factory had so yearned to be sent," wrote biographer Michael Slater. "To complicate matters still further, the young Scrooge's desolate and decaying schoolhouse, 'a mansion of dull red brick, with a little weather-cock-surmounted cupola, on the roof,' recalls Gad's Hill Place as seen from the outside. The forsaken-child image of the young Dickens sits, deprived of hope but comforted by imaginative literature, in the ruins of his own dream home."

From their home at St. Mary's Place, Fanny and Charles could see out over the church and its steeple, as well as the graveyard nearby. Dickens recalled this time in Chatham in a small story, "A Child's Dream of a Star," which many scholars feel reflects the closeness of the two in childhood. He wrote:

"There was one clear shining star that used to come out in the sky before the rest, near the church spire, above the graves. It was larger and more beautiful, they thought, than all others, and every night they watched for it, standing hand in hand at the window. Whoever saw it first, cried out, 'I see the star!' And often they cried out both together, knowing so well when it would rise, and where. So they grew to be such friends with it, that before lying down in their beds, they always looked out once again, to bid it good night; and when they were turning around to sleep, they used to say, 'God bless the star!' "

Dickens biographer Peter Ackroyd pointed out: "Those who seek reasons for the ubiquity of that name [Fanny] in his fiction might start their search here. . . . On that criterion alone his response to the name is, to say the least, somewhat ambiguous; there is Fanny Dombey, the doomed mother of little Paul who dies in childbirth, but then of course there is also Fanny Squeers, the grotesque and ugly daughter of the famous Yorkshire schoolmaster. And then—in between, as it were—there is Fanny Dorrit, the imperious and petulant elder sister of Little Dorrit. There are also eight other characters who bear the same name. Now there is no doubt that Dickens did use Christian names which for some reason were emblematic for him—that is why the names of his father and sister crop up so often—and there is no doubt, too, that this was on occasions a deliberate device. But the range of Fannies in his fiction is so great that it suggests at the very least a most complicated relationship with his sibling. But we know also that, for Dickens himself, the relationship between brother and sister became the paradigm for human relationships in general; that loving sexless union of siblings is commemorated again and again in his novels."

He was not reading now, but walking up and down despairingly. Scrooge looked at the Ghost, and with a mournful shaking of his head, glanced anxiously towards the door.

It opened; and a little girl, much younger than the boy, came darting in, and putting her arms about his neck, and often kissing him, addressed him as her "Dear, dear brother."

"I have come to bring you home, dear brother!" said the child, clapping her tiny hands, and bending down to laugh. "To bring you home, home, home!"

When the Dickens family was reposted to London, Charles stayed behind with Mr. Giles a little while longer. He probably left Chatham around Christmas time 1822 or the early part of 1823.

"*Home, little Fan?*" *returned the boy.*

"*Yes!*" *said the child, brimful of glee.* "*Home, for good and all. Home, for ever and ever. Father is so much kinder than he used to be, that home's like Heaven! He spoke so gently to me one dear night when I was going to bed, that I was not afraid to ask him once more if you might come home; and he said Yes, you should; and sent me in a coach to bring you. And you're to be a man!*" *said the child, opening her eyes,* "*and are never to come back here. . . .*"

The night before he left the school, Mr. Giles "came fitting among the packing cases, to give me Goldsmith's Bee as a keepsake. Which I kept for his sake, and its own, a long while afterwards."

On leaving Chatham, Dickens later recounted, ". . . in the days when there were no railroads in the land, I left it in a stage coach. Through all of the years that have since passed have I ever lost the smell of the damp straw in which I was packed—like game—and forwarded. . . . There was no other inside passenger, and I consumed my sandwiches in solitude and dreariness, and it rained hard all the way. . . ."

For Dickens these memories were not easy ones to choke down, knowing that his departure from Giles' school would be more bittersweet than he could suppose at the time. The Dickenses had moved to Camden Town.

Old Fezziwig

The Ghost stopped at a certain warehouse door, and asked Scrooge if he knew it.

"Know it!" said Scrooge. "Was I apprenticed here!"

They went in. At sight of an old gentleman in a Welsh wig, sitting behind such a high desk, that if he had been two inches taller he must have knocked his head against the ceiling, Scrooge cried in great excitement:

"Why, it's old Fezziwig! Bless his heart; it's Fezziwig alive again!"

There are two very important character traits to know about Fezziwig—he's a responsible businessman and he loves to dance. For Scrooge it is of immense importance to relive his time at Fezziwig's

business. It is an absolutely necessary part of his reclamation. And for Dickens' own part, he too loved to dance.

> *Then old Fezziwig stood out to dance with Mrs.*
> *Fezziwig. Top couple, too; with a good stiff piece of work*
> *cut out for them; three or four and twenty pair of partners;*
> *people who were not to be trifled with; people who would*
> *dance, and had no notion of walking.*
> *But if they had been twice as many—ah, four times—*
> *old Fezziwig would have been a match for them, and so*
> *would Mrs. Fezziwig.*

"When we were only babies my father determined that
we should be taught to dance, so as early as the Genoa
days we were given our first lessons," recalled Mamie
Dickens in her memoir *My Father, As I Recall Him.* " 'Our
oldest boy and his sisters are to be waited upon next week
by a professor of the noble art of dancing,' [my father]
wrote to a friend at this time. And again, in writing to
my mother, he says: 'I hope the dancing lessons will be a
success. Don't fail to let me know.'

"Our progress in the graceful art delighted him, and
his admiration of our success was evident when we
exhibited to him, as we were perfected in them, all the
steps, exercises and dances which formed our lessons.
He always encouraged us in our dancing, and praised
our grace and aptness, although criticized quite severely

in some places for allowing his children to expend so much time and energy upon the training of their feet," continued Mamie.

The portrait of Old Fezziwig from the title page
of the first edition of A Christmas Carol.

"When 'the boys' came home for the holidays there were constant rehearsals for the Christmas and New Year's parties; and more especially for the dance on Twelfth Night, the anniversary of my brother Charlie's birthday. Just before one of these celebrations my father insisted that my sister Katie and I should teach the polka step to Mr. Leech and himself. My father was as much in earnest about learning to take that wonderful step correctly, as though there were nothing of greater importance in the world. Often he would practice gravely in a corner, without either partner or music, and I remember one cold winter's night his awakening with the fear that he had forgotten the step so strong upon him that, jumping out of bed, by the scant illumination of the old-fashioned rushlight, and to his own whistling, he diligently rehearsed its 'one, two, three, one, two, three' until he was once more secure in his knowledge.

"No one can imagine our excitement and nervousness when the evening came on which we were to dance with our pupils. Katie was to have Mr. Leech, who was over six feet tall, for her partner, while my father was to be mine. My heart beat so fast that I could scarcely breathe, I was so fearful for the success of our exhibition. But my fears were groundless, and we were greeted at the finish of our dance with hearty applause, which was more than compensation for the work which had been expended upon its learning.

"My father was certainly not what in the ordinary acceptation of the term would be called 'a good dancer.' I doubt whether he had ever received any instruction in 'the noble art' other than that which my sister and I gave him. In later years I remember trying to teach him the Schottische, a dance which he particularly admired and desired to learn. But although he was so fond of dancing, except at family gatherings in his own or his most inti-mate friends' homes, I never remember seeing him join in it himself, and I doubt if, even as a young man, he ever went to balls. Graceful in motion, his dancing, such as it was, was natural to him. Dance music was delightful to his cheery, genial spirit; the time and steps of a dance suited his tidy nature, if I may so speak. The action and the exercise seemed to be a part of his abundant vitality," she fondly recalled.

"His dancing was at its best, I think, in the 'Sir Roger de Coverly' . . . and in what are known as country dances. In the former, while the end couples are dancing, and the side couples are supposed to be still, my father would insist upon the sides keeping up a kind of jig step, and clapping his hands to add to the fun, and dancing at the backs of those whose enthusiasm he thought needed rousing, was himself never still for a moment until the dance was over. He was very fond of a country dance which he learned at the house of some dear friends at Rockingham Castle, which began with quite a stately minuet to the tune of

'God save the Queen,' and then dashed suddenly into 'Down the Middle and up Again.' His enthusiasm in this dance, I remember, was so great that, one evening after some of our Tavistock House theatricals, when I was thoroughly worn out with fatigue, being selected by him as his partner, I caught the infection of his merriment, and my weariness vanished. As he himself says, in describing dear old 'Fezziwig's' Christmas party, we were 'people who would dance and had no notion of walking.' "

But for Scrooge, the difference in his relationship with his old master Fezziwig is in strong contrast to his relationship with Cratchit. "The relationship between the youthful Scrooge and his master, Old Fezziwig, had been a paternalist one. Scrooge was Fezziwig's apprentice, not his employee," wrote Stephen Nissenbaum. "But as Dickens himself well knew, that was in an earlier age in a precapitalist culture. The economic system had changed, and with it the social relationships between patron and client."

So, for Dickens, Fezziwig represented the old way things were done, and how heartless he found the employer/employee relationship in this new industrial age. Fezziwig eats at Christmas with his employees. Scrooge and his class do not.

Belle

"It matters little," she said, softly. "To you, very little. Another idol has displaced me; and if it can cheer and comfort you in time to come, as I would have tried to do, I have no just cause to grieve."

ickens watched Scrooge weather this first ghost, reviewing his past as it were, as Scrooge was experiencing a kind of baptism by fire. It is in these moments that Dickens understood that we all needed to see bits of Scrooge's humanity, and that the audience needed to understand how society and the unrestrained industrialization of Britain had whittled Scrooge down to the deep, nasty point where he now found himself.

Dickens was thirty-two years old and saddled with the debts of not only his own making but that of his parents and several siblings. He had seen even in himself how circumstances can make one slowly lose the enthusiasms of youth in the responsibilities of adulthood.

Indeed, Dickens saw a bit of himself in Scrooge, as all men and women are supposed to. Like Scrooge as a young adult, Dickens at the time was a young man whose career was just about to take off and, overwhelmed with work, he took for granted his relationship with fiancee Catherine Hogarth.

After a failed tempestuous romance with a young woman named Maria Beadnell, another young lady, Catherine Hogarth, daughter of fellow reporter George Hogarth, caught Dickens' eye. He was in love. And he put himself on full display for her.

Dickens had fond memories of their courtship. But there seems little doubt that Scrooge's interlude with Belle came from somewhere in Dickens' past.

George Hogarth worked for *The Morning Chronicle* as a writer on political and musical subjects, and was later named the editor of *The Evening Chronicle*. It was Hogarth who had commissioned Dickens to write a series of stories under the pseudonym "Boz." The two became friendly, and Hogarth invited the young Dickens to his home.

As Dickens chronicler Claire Tomalin wrote, "Hogarth . . . had a large and still growing family, and when he

[Dickens] made his first visit to their house on the
Fulham Road, surrounded by gardens and orchards, he
met their eldest daughter, nineteen-year-old Catherine.
Her unaffectedness appealed to him at once, along with
the fact that she was different from the young woman
he had recently known, not only in being Scottish but
in coming from an educated family with literary connec-
tions. The Hogarths, like the Beadnells, were a cut above
the Dickens family, but they welcomed Dickens warmly
as an equal, and George Hogarth's enthusiasm for his
work was flattering."

Catherine Dickens.

One of the daughters, Georgina Hogarth, later recalled
that on one occasion, Dickens "dressed as a sailor jumped
in at the window, danced a hornpipe, whistling the tune
jumped out again, and a few minutes later Dickens walked

gravely in at the door, as if nothing had happened, shook hands all round, and then, at the sight of their puzzled faces, burst into a roar of laughter."

Tomalin continued, "He saw in her the affection, compliance and physical pleasure, and he believed he was in love with her. That was enough for him to ask her to be his wife. . . ."

In the fall of 1835, Dickens was over-committed. He still had a day job as a reporter, and was writing fiction on the side that would soon make him a literary superstar. If there was anything that Dickens wanted so much, it was financial and emotional security. His burgeoning career and Catherine Hogarth were both right before him. The demands of the publishers he had committed to were looming. He had in fact over-burdened himself. The juggling of these two overriding ambitions—money and love—were set to work against each other.

"I am writing by candle-light shivering with cold, and choked with smoke," he told one friend, and related to yet another, "My Laundress who is asthmatic, has dived into a closet . . . and is emitting from behind a closet door an uninterrupted succession of the most unearthly and hollow noises I have ever heard."

"All the while he was trying to balance the needs of his career against his duties to Catherine, who, on occasions, seems to have been disturbed by his attention to his work at the expense of herself. It was not unreasonable for her to be so: it must have looked as if this was the shape their marriage was about to take, and indeed she was not mistaken," wrote biographer Peter Ackroyd.

"Though she was pettily possessive and resentful of what she felt was his neglect he repeatedly begged her not to blame him," wrote Norman and Jeanne MacKenzie. "Almost every letter Dickens sent Kate during the winter months was an explanation, an apology, or an assurance intended to mollify her."

Apologizing to Kate in one note, for yet another missed engagement, Dickens wrote, "You know . . . I have frequently wrote you that my composition is peculiar. I can never write with effect—especially in a serious way—until I have got my steam up, or in other words until I have become so excited with my subject that I cannot leave off."

"Kate," wrote Edgar Johnson, "finding that all these demands upon Dickens' time kept him away from her, began to feel neglected and aggrieved. She complained of being in 'low spirits' and tried to make him sorry for her by saying in . . . a childish pout that she was 'cross,' reiterating that he could come to see her if he would and that he took pleasure in being away."

Dickens tried to reason with his unhappy and lonely Kate, writing, "You may be disappointed—I would rather you would—at not seeing me, but you cannot feel vexed at my doing my best with the stake I have to play for—you and a home for the both of us." Even as he was writing, Dickens' father was finding himself in financial straits again.

But Dickens could come across seemingly harsh when he wrote her, at one point unhappy with his own literary output one evening, asserting that "the quantity is not sufficient to justify my coming out tonight. If the representations I have so often made to you, about my working as a duty, and not as a pleasure, be not sufficient to keep you in a good humor, which you, of all people in the world should preserve—why then, my dear, you must be out of temper, and there is no help for it."

But Scrooge and Dickens do diverge. Dickens, for his part, took a room not far from Kate's house so it would be easier to see her. He made the commitment necessary for them to marry. To him, Kate and her family symbolized the kind of security he had not known as a child.

Scrooge, on the other hand, does not see the folly of his way until it is too late. Accompanied by the Ghost of Christmas Past, Scrooge relives the moment that Belle let him go forever:

> ". . . *if you were free to-day, to-morrow, yesterday, can even I believe that you would choose a dowerless girl—you who, in your very confidence with her, weigh everything by Gain: or, choosing her, if for a moment you were false enough to your one guiding principle to do so, do I not know that your repentance and regret would surely follow?*

*I do; and I release you. With a full heart, for the love of
him you once were. . . .*

"May you be happy in the life you have chosen!"
She left him, and they parted.
*"Spirit!" said Scrooge, "show me no more! Conduct
me home. Why do you delight to torture me?"*

Scrooge is obviously saddened by these images. But
his utter failure as a human being is shown in the last
scene with Belle. The spirit shows a young girl sitting in a
room, and Scrooge believes the girl is Belle. As his vision
sharpens, he realizes that the girl is Belle's daughter, and
that Bella, a woman now, resides over a happy home filled
with children and commotion. The scene is Christmas
Eve, and Belle's husband arrives with a man in tow whose
arms are filled to the brim with presents. The children
clamor for their booty.

*"Belle," said the husband, turning to his wife with
a smile, "I saw an old friend of yours this afternoon."*
"Who was it?"
"Guess!"
*"How can I? Tut, don't I know?" she added in the same
breath, laughing as he laughed. "Mr. Scrooge."*
*"Mr. Scrooge it was. I passed his office window; and
as it was not shut up, and he had a candle inside, I could
scarcely help seeing him. His partner lies upon the point of*

death, I hear; and there he sat alone. Quite alone in the world, I do believe."

Scrooge's aloneness was now complete. His life was confirmed as an utter desolation.

Dickens was now completely taken by *A Christmas Carol*, obsessed with it as Forster recalled later, "with what a strange mastery it seized him for itself, how he wept over it, and laughed, and wept again, and excited himself to an extraordinary degree, and how he walked thinking of it fifteen and twenty miles about the black streets of London, many and many a night after all sober folks had gone to bed."

It is no wonder he wept and laughed and wept again. As much as Ebenezer Scrooge was taken back and forth in time, so would Dickens visit many of the good and sad times of his own life and confront his own ghosts and demons more bluntly than he had ever attempted to do so. This little book would bring back shameful, hurtful memories, as well as great smiles. It was to be a heroic private battle with his own past that he would not talk about to his last days.

Stave III

The Ghost
of Christmas Present

The moment Scrooge's hand was on the lock, a strange voice called him by his name, and bade him enter. He obeyed.

It was his own room. There was no doubt about that. But it had undergone a surprising transformation. The walls and ceiling were so hung with living green, that it looked a perfect grove; from every part of which, bright gleaming berries glistened. The crisp leaves of holly, mistletoe, and ivy reflected back the light, as if so many little mirrors had been scattered there; and such a mighty blaze went roaring up the chimney, as that dull petrification of a hearth had never known in Scrooge's time, or Marley's, or for many and many a *winter season gone. Heaped up on the floor, to form a kind of throne, were turkeys, geese, game, poultry, brawn, great joints of meat, sucking-pigs, long wreaths of sausages, mince-pies, plum-puddings, barrels of oysters, red-hot chestnuts, cherry-cheeked apples, juicy oranges, luscious pears, immense twelfth-cakes, and seething bowls of punch, that made the chamber dim with their delicious steam. In easy state upon this couch, there sat a jolly Giant, glorious to see: who bore a glowing torch, in shape not unlike Plenty's horn, and held it up, high up, to shed its light on Scrooge, as he came peeping round the door.*

By the first week of November 1843 Dickens was excited about his progress in the story. He and Forster were going back and forth. He had been juggling writing the installments for *Martin Chuzzlewit* while also writing *Carol*.

Dickens was still trying to figure out how to pull away from his publishers Chapman and Hall. He remained angry at them for numerous failures (some of which were real, some imagined, and some brought on by his constant want of money), and was determined to no longer be at their mercy. He owed them money since they had lent him large advances, all of which had not earned out.

"I am bent on paying the money," Dickens had ranted

to Forster in June 1843. He had been courted by other publishers, and Bradbury and Evans were the favored ones. Dickens proposed buying back all the rights to his books and then reselling them to the next publisher. He had been absolutely stunned that his current publishers had suggested cheap editions of his novels while he was still at the height of his fame, a fame which seemed was slowly slipping after his long absence in America and with the troublesome publishing of *Martin Chuzzlewit.*

"And before going into the matter with anybody I should like you to propound from me the one preliminary question to Bradbury and Evans. It is more than a year and a half since Clowes wrote to urge me to give him a hearing, in case I should ever think of altering my plans. A printer is better than a bookseller, and it is quite as much the interest of one (if not more) to join me. But whoever it is, or whatever, I am bent upon paying Chapman and Hall *down.* And when I have done that, Mr. Hall shall have a piece of my mind."

Forster had hoped Dickens' ire would fade. But Dickens' letter of November 1, 1843 put that to bed. Dickens at this point was in earnest when he wrote to Forster to tell him that he absolutely intended to write, produce, and publish the book himself. Forster was flabbergasted.

"Don't be startled by the novelty and extent of my project," Dickens wrote. "Both startled *me* at first; but I am well assured of its wisdom and necessity. I am afraid of a magazine—just now. I don't think the time a good one, or the chances favorable. I am afraid of putting myself before the town as writing tooth and nail for bread, head-long, after the close of a book taking so much out of one as *Chuzzlewit*. I am afraid I could not do it, with justice to myself. I know that whatever we may say at first, a new magazine, or a new anything, would require so much propping, that I should be forced (as in the Clock) to put myself into it, in my old shape. I am afraid of Bradbury and Evans's desire to force on the cheap issue of my books, or any of them, prematurely. I am sure if it took place yet awhile, it would damage me and damage the property, enormously. It is very natural in them to want it; but, since they do want it, I have no faith in their regarding me in any other respect than they would regard any other man in a speculation. I see that this is really your opinion as well; and I don't see what I gain, in such a case, by leaving Chapman and Hall. . . . At the close of *Chuzzlewit* (by which time the debt will have been mate-rially reduced) I purpose drawing from Chapman and Hall my share of the subscription—bills, or money, will do equally well. I design to tell them that it is not likely I shall do anything for a year; that, in the meantime, I make no arrangement whatever with any one; and our business matters rest in status quo. The same to Bradbury and Evans."

"There were difficulties, still to be strongly urged,

against taking any present step to a final resolve; and he gave way a little," Forster related.

"I have been, all day in *Chuzzlewit* agonies—conceiving only. I hope to bring forth to-morrow," Dickens wrote Forster on November 10, "I want to say a word or two about the cover of the *Carol* and the advertising, and to consult you on a nice point in the tale."

But Dickens pressed Forster again, writing, "And do, my dear fellow, do for God's sake turn over about Chapman and Hall, and look upon my project as a settled thing. If you object to see them, I must write to them."

Forster convinced Dickens to delay. As Edgar Johnson rightly pointed out, "Chapman and Hall were publishing A *Christmas Carol* on commission for Dickens; that announcement that Dickens was quitting them at such time would foolishly jeopardize the little book's chances."

With all this swirling in his head, Dickens was now turning to the highpoint of the story. Things here must highlight the direst of circumstances. His walking did not abate. As the book began to near the end of its story, Dickens made more and more preparations for its publication. He hired John Leech to illustrate the title, and agreed to print the book himself, so sure was he of its success (and of his publisher's inabilities based on the lackluster sales of *Martin Chuzzlewit*).

Dickens pressed on with *Chuzzlewit* and *Carol*.

"Come in!" exclaimed the Ghost. "Come in! and know me better, man!"

Abundance was the signature of the Christmas season for Dickens. And he loved no more abundance than food at Christmas time. Dickens himself was not an over indulger, but the symbolism of it to him was paramount. A respite from the world's cares and worries, in a moment of enjoyment, jollity, and rest. He loved Christmas.

Dickens was obsessed with his little book, and when John Leech—the celebrated *Punch* magazine illustrator he had hired—showed him the original hand-tinted illustrations of the Ghost of Christmas Present, Dickens objected to the color of the ghost's robe; Leech had tinted the robe red. Copies of the illustration exist to this day at the Pierpont Morgan Library. Dickens had described the robe as green in the text, but had Leech taken literary license or was it just a mistake? Nonetheless, Dickens corrected it, and in the final edition the robe was correctly colored green. But these were the kinds of details that were not escaping Dickens despite his massive creative commitments.

"Leech was a nervous, easily offended artist, and Dickens must have taken pains to please and appease him," wrote historian Hearn.

The final version of John Leech's illustration
of the Ghost of Christmas Present.

There was no mistake that Dickens loved Covent Garden. He walked there often. He found its abundance, though, was tarnished, and it was this very thing that Dickens next shared with his readers. The first scene of Stave III was set in the major market of the Old City.

Dickens had first read about Covent Garden Market in George Coleman's *Broad Grins* in 1822, which inspired him to come see the market when he was ten years old.

"When I had money enough I used to go to a coffee-shop, and have a half-a-pint of coffee and a slice of bread and butter. When I had no money I took a turn in Covent Garden Market and stared at the pineapples," Dickens later remembered of his youth when he worked in a factory where he placed labels on pots of boot black.

Covent Garden.

"Constantly underfed, Charles sniffed hungrily at the food in the London stores and streets. He played mental games whether to buy one type of pudding or another or to buy attractive food now and have no money later, or to buy attractive food later and have no food now, or to act like a grown up and plan sensibly," wrote biographer Fred Kaplan. Regardless, the market was a bonanza that appealed to Dickens his whole life, and these early childhood experiences stuck with him.

The first record of a "new market in Covent Garden" was in 1654 when market traders set up stalls against the garden wall of Bedford House. The Earl of Bedford acquired a private charter from Charles II in 1670 for a fruit and vegetable market, permitting him and his heirs to hold a market every day except Sunday and Christmas Day. The original market, consisting of wooden stalls and sheds, became disorganized and disorderly with rampant crime and widespread prostitution, and the 6th Earl requested an Act of Parliament in 1813 to regulate it, then commissioned Charles Fowler in 1830 to design the neoclassical market building that is the heart of Covent Garden today. With the new buildings and the new laws surrounding it, the market enjoyed a better (even if it did not have shining) reputation by the time Dickens was walking about in 1844. Still, there was nothing that compared with the abundance with which the market sparkled.

Dickens described his mornings in the garden, writing, "There was early coffee to be got about Covent-garden Market, and that was more company—warm company, too, which was better. Toast of a very substantial quality, was likewise procurable: though the towzled-headed man who made it, in an inner chamber within the coffee-room, hadn't got his coat on yet, and was so heavy with sleep that in every interval of toast and coffee he went off anew behind the partition into complicated cross-roads of choke and snore, and lost his way directly."

In the beginning of Stave III, Dickens catalogued the many foods available. "The poulterers' shops were still half open, and the fruiterers' were radiant in their glory. There were great, round, pot-bellied baskets of chestnuts, shaped like the waistcoats of jolly old gentlemen, lolling at the doors, and tumbling out into the street in their apoplectic opulence. There were ruddy, brown-faced, broad-girthed Spanish Onions, shining in the fatness of their growth like Spanish Friars. . . . There were pears and

apples, clustered high in blooming pyramids; there were
bunches of grapes . . . there were piles of filberts, mossy
and brown, recalling, in their fragrance, ancient walks
among the woods . . . setting off the yellow of the oranges
and lemons. . . ."

Dickens mentioned sticks of "cinnamon so long and
straight, the other spices so delicious, the candied fruits
so caked and spotted with molten sugar as to make the
coldest lookers-on feel faint and subsequently bilious."

> . . . *on the threshold of the door the Spirit smiled, and*
> *stopped to bless Bob Cratchit's dwelling with the sprinkling*
> *of his torch. Think of that! Bob had but fifteen "Bob"*
> *a-week himself; he pocketed on Saturdays but fifteen copies*
> *of his Christian name; and yet the Ghost of Christmas*
> *Present blessed his four-roomed house!*

But this blessing—though Dickens himself wrote it—
was difficult for him to face, for the Cratchits *were* none
other than the Dickens family when they'd just moved to
London, just before their father went into debtors' prison.
Yet the memories of Bayham Street were all painful ones
for Dickens.

Remembering years later the loss of innocence in this
period, with the ultimate imprisonment of his father and
his being sent off to factory work, Dickens wrote, ". . .
I fell into a state of neglect, which I have never been able

to look back on without a kind of agony."

But in the Cratchits, he tried to paint a more stiff-upper lip, more optimistic portrait of his youth. While in Dickens' mind his family's days spent on Bayham were awful, he painted the Cratchits as downtrodden but not beaten. They were the heroic working class.

Dickens' own memories were less optimistic.

"I know that we got on very badly with the butcher and the baker, and that very often we had not too much to eat," Dickens recalled of their time at Bayham Street. He wrote of his father that ". . . I degenerated into cleaning his boots of a morning, and my own; and making myself useful in the work of the little house; and looking after my younger brothers and sisters (we were now six in all); and going on such poor errands as arose out of a poor way of living."

There were eight people altogether in the four-room house—his father and mother, John and Elizabeth, and in order of their birth: Fanny, Charles, Letitia, Harriet, Frederick, and Alfred.

"Workers with some income, could do better," wrote Victorian historian Daniel Poole about housing in that period, "and a clerk like Bob Cratchit, at the bottom of the middle class, characteristically might enjoy a small four-room house in a London suburb like Camdentown with one room for the kitchen, one for a dining room-parlor, and the other two for bedrooms."

As an adult, Dickens threw himself into Christmas, but ". . . others observed that Dickens' enjoyment of Christmas seemed more determined, even ruthless, than one might expect from someone with a genuinely boyish sense of fun," wrote Robert Douglas-Fairhurst, a Dickens expert. "Perhaps his memories of Warren's Blacking were to blame. His family's accounts certainly suggest an attempt on Dickens' part to re-create his childhood as it should have been, rather than as it was. His fiction too reveals surprisingly mixed feelings over Christmas as a time of peace and joy. For all its versions of plum puddings and mistletoe, and all that readers have come to think of Dickens as literature's answer to Santa Claus, he rarely describes a family Christmas without showing how vulnerable it is to being broken apart by a more miserable alternative."

> *Then up rose Mrs. Cratchit, Cratchit's wife, dressed out but poorly in a twice-turned gown, but brave in ribbons, which are cheap and make a goodly show for sixpence; and she laid the cloth, assisted by Belinda Cratchit, second of her daughters, also brave in ribbons; while Master Peter Cratchit plunged a fork into the saucepan of potatoes, and getting the corners of his monstrous shirt collar (Bob's private property, conferred upon his son and heir in honor of the day) into his mouth, rejoiced to find himself so gallantly attired, and yearned to show his linen in the fashionable Parks.*

And now two smaller Cratchits, boy and girl, came tearing in, screaming that outside the baker's they had smelt the goose, and known it for their own; and basking in luxurious thoughts of sage and onion, these young Cratchits danced about the table, and exalted Master Peter Cratchit to the skies, while he (not proud, although his collars nearly choked him) blew the fire, until the slow potatoes bubbling up, knocked loudly at the saucepan-lid to be let out and peeled.

"That image of everyone sitting around the table with a great big goose—this is when it comes about, in the 1830s and 1840s," says Alex Werner, a senior curator of social and working history at the Museum of London.

"Narrative snapshots like the Cratchits' happy family Christmas may linger in the memory, but in Dickens' fictional world they are set against a background where the domestic ideal is far more likely to be flaking around the edges," concluded Douglas-Fairhurst.

This tenderness of scene, this simple show of home and hearth and goodwill amongst the Cratchits, is what endeared the Cratchits, and by extension, Dickens, to readers since the story's publication.

Tiny Tim

"And how did little Tim behave?" asked Mrs. Cratchit.
. . .

"As good as gold," said Bob, "and better. Somehow he gets thoughtful, sitting by himself so much, and thinks the strangest things you ever heard. He told me, coming home, that he hoped the people saw him in the church, because he was a cripple, and it might be pleasant to them to remember upon Christmas Day, who made lame beggars walk, and blind men see."

Now Dickens would introduce a new character. A little boy. As Dickens began to write of the little handicapped boy he had conjured, he was not sure for whom he would name the character. Originally he named him "Little Fred." Dickens may have been thinking of his younger sibling Alfred, who had died in childhood. But he later decided to name Scrooge's nephew Fred, and so he later scratched out "Little Fred" for "Tiny Mick" for a time, but ultimately settled on "Tiny Tim."

Who was Timothy Cratchit? In reality, Tiny Tim as we know him today was an amalgamation of two different people.

Dickens' sister Fanny had a disabled son named Henry Burnett Jr. also called Harry. Tiny Tim did not receive his name from Fanny's child, but the aspects of Tiny Tim's character are taken from Henry Burnett Jr.

Henry Burnett Jr. was born in 1839 in Manchester. According to Dickens biographer Fred Kaplan, "Franny's crippled eldest son, who always had a fragile hold on life, seemed unlikely to outlive his mother by much, if at all." At the time of the writing of A Christmas Carol, Henry would have been five years old. There is no doubt Henry was one of the inspirations for Tim. And ultimately, he was the inspiration for Paul Dombey Jr. in Dombey and Son.

According to the Reverend James Griffin of Manchester, "Harry was a singular child—meditative and quaint in a remarkable degree. He was the original, as Mr. Dickens told his sister, of little 'Paul Dombey.' Harry had been taken to Brighton . . . for hours lying on the beach with his books, given utterance to thoughts quite as remarkable for a child. . . ." Like many Dickens biographers, Peter Ackroyd suggested that Harry "had also suggested to his famous uncle the character of Tiny Tim."

It has also been claimed that the character is based on the son of a friend of Dickens who owned a cotton mill in Ardwick, Manchester, in the same town as Fanny's sister. Ardwick was a tony suburb of Manchester in Dickens' time, with three cotton mills in operation before 1850.

With these little-known facts, still, Tiny Tim has been a character in fiction that has endured almost outside of *A Christmas Carol.* And of course, the question foremost on everyone's mind is this: What was Tiny Tim's illness?

Alas for Tiny Tim, he bore a little crutch, and had his limbs supported by an iron frame!

For more than a century, doctors have discussed a multitude of possible diseases for Tiny Tim. Dickens left us few clues, but enough for Russell Chesney, a physician at Le Bonheur Children's Hospital at the University of Tennessee Health Science Center in Memphis, who published his finding in March 2012 to great fanfare in a journal published by the American Medical Association. According to Dr. Chesney, Tiny Tim suffered from a combination of rickets and tuberculosis.

Chesney made his diagnosis based on Tim's deformities described in the text, along with the story's insinuation that the boy's disease would be curable if his father had more money. Rickets is a bone disorder caused by a deficiency in vitamin D, calcium, or phosphate. Lack of these crucial nutrients softens the bones, and leg braces would have been the 1840s solution, Chesney said. Since vitamin D-fortified milk and infant formula was introduced decades ago, this disorder is rarely seen in the United States today.

According to Chesney, "The blackened skies would have prevented skin synthesis of vitamin D, and Tiny Tim's chances of having rickets were substantial. . . . Because the ash blocked UV-B rays, it could have contributed to insufficient sunlight exposure for children in London in the time of Tiny Tim, in the 1820s." There is no question that Manchester was an industry town of the ilk Dr. Chesney alludes to, and probably thus burdened the two boys who were models for Tiny Tim with at least one of the two afflictions considered.

"The salary earned by Bob Cratchit would have influenced the diet available to Tiny Tim. The 4 one-pound loaves of bread that 15 shillings would buy may have been adulterated with alum [hydrated potassium aluminum sulfate] to whiten the bread and disguise the use of poor quality flour. Alum is used today as an antiperspirant, in styptic pencils, in baking powder, and as a pickling agent in many cuisines but was added to bread throughout the 19th century in London. It, like other aluminum salts used as antacids, can bind phosphate in the intestine and prevent its absorption," reasoned Dr. Chesney.

Even if Mrs. Cratchit had made her own bread, the likelihood of Tim having rickets was high. Chesney made the assertion that at that time, sixty percent of children of working-class London families had rickets. So this is not a stretch to say Tim probably had rickets, whether Dickens knew it or not.

"People who have nutritional deficiency also may have diseases in which nutrition plays a role, and tuberculosis is one of them," Chesney explained.

But why the enduring appeal of a sickly child?

"As the economy shifted from an agricultural base to one dependent on industrial manufacturing, people with disabilities were increasingly assumed to be 'useless' non-producers, 'invalids' who were not capable of participating in the economy. But a function was discovered for them in this secularized system—a function most perfectly fulfilled by Charles Dickens' figure of Tiny Tim," according to the radio program "Inventing the Poster Child" from NPR (National Public Radio), produced by Laurie Block with Jay Allison, which proclaimed Tim the first "poster child."

"The dependent person with a disability—especially the child—was able to awaken the heart of Economic Man (Scrooge) and soften the iron laws of economics. Though the laws cannot be abrogated, charitable feelings can be exercised outside their sphere. Public philanthropy directed toward those who fall out of the economic equation is the secular version of longstanding Christian charitable imperatives directed toward the poor and helpless in general. The dependent person with a disability—Tiny Tim—has no independent character in this drama. In this tale, there is no possibility that a person with a disability might be able to have an independent economic function if adaptations are made. Nor does Tiny Tim have the option of refusing the charity he inspires. Tiny Tim's innocent goodness, helplessness, and cheerful acceptance of his 'affliction' remind some people with disabilities of Harriet Beecher Stowe's near-contemporaneous Uncle Tom," concluded the NPR broadcast.

The Miners

And now, without a word of warning from the Ghost,
they stood upon a bleak and desert moor. . . .
"What place is this?" asked Scrooge.
"A place where Miners live, who labour in the bowels of
the earth," returned the Spirit. "But they know me. See!"

ickens for some reason had become obsessed with
visiting Cornwall. He had written to friend John
Forster that he had an idea to start a story there,
set in a lighthouse on the rough Cornwall coast, and see
"some terribly dreary iron-bound spot . . . we will then
together fly down into that desolate region."

"From October 27, to 4 November 1842, Dickens and
his friends toured Cornwall in an open carriage amid

much jollity and boisterous fun. Dickens later described .
. . their exploration of 'earthy old churches' and 'strange
caverns on the gloomy seashore' as well as their going
'down into the depths of Mines. . . ,' " recorded biographer
Michael Slater.

Dickens later abandoned the idea of using Cornwall
for a story setting, according to Slater, but "his imagination continued to be haunted by its rugged landscape,
mines, and dramatic coastline. They appear in the
Carol, for example, when Scrooge finds himself trans-
ported to 'a bleak and desert moor, where monstrous
masses of rude stone were cast about as though it were
the burial place of giants,' and then whirled out to sea
where his ears are 'deafened by the thundering of water,
as it rolled, roared, and raged among the dreadful caverns it had worn, and fiercely tried to undermine
the earth.' "

From there, the ghost takes Scrooge to the lighthouse
Dickens had always envisioned, with a few solitary figures
standing within the thick, heavy walls of the lighthouse,
with weather and water raging all around and the yellow-
orange glow of the fire proving safe inside. This was all
locked up for safekeeping by Dickens in 1842, and was
now spilt out onto his pages.

"He's a comical old fellow," said Scrooge's nephew,
"that's the truth: and not so pleasant as he might be.

However, his offences carry their own punishment, and I have nothing to say against him."

With the holiday season coming up, Dickens put on himself not only the immense pressure of writing, producing, and publishing his own book, he still put pressure on himself to learn a new dance or parlor trick for the season's festivities. And of course, he loved parlor games.

Charles Dickens in 1842.

"Christmas was always a time which in our home was looked forward to with eagerness and delight," recalled Catherine and Charles' daughter Mamie many years later. His son Henry recalled that Christmas in their home "was a great time, a really jovial time, and my father was always at his best, a splendid host, bright and jolly as a boy and throwing his heart and soul into everything that was going on."

"Our Christmas Day dinners at 'Gad's Hill' were particularly bright and cheery, some of our nearest neighbors joining our home party. The Christmas plum pudding had its own special dish of colored 'repoussé' china, ornamented with holly. The pudding was placed on this with a sprig of real holly in the centre, lighted, and in this state placed in front of my father, its arrival being always the signal for applause. A prettily decorated table was his special pleasure, and from my earliest girlhood the care of this devolved upon me. When I had everything in readiness, he would come with me to inspect the result of my labors, before dressing for dinner, and no word except of praise ever came to my ears," recalled Mamie Dickens years later.

"He was a wonderfully neat and rapid carver, and I am happy to say taught me some of his skill in this. I used to help him in our home parties at 'Gad's Hill' by carving at a side table, returning to my seat opposite him as soon as my duty was ended," remembered Mamie Dickens.

She ended her holiday remembrances with, "Supper was served, the hot mulled wine drunk in toasts, and the maddest and wildest of 'Sir Roger de Coverlys' ended our evening. . . ." Of course, during the Christmas season, he loved to imbibe. So much so that he eventually created his own holiday punch, like the lord of an old English manner. Punch and flips were both big in those days, and Dickens was no stranger to their appeal.

Below is Charles Dickens' own recipe for a punch. It is sourced from a letter Dickens wrote on January 18, 1847, to Amelia Austin Filloneau, affectionately known as "Mrs. F." This punch may be served warm or cold, as noted. The recipe is in his own words.

CHARLES DICKENS' PUNCH RECIPE

3 lemons rinds

1 cup sugar

1 pint rum

½ pint brandy

1 quart water (boiling)

1. Peel into a very strong common basin the rinds of three lemons, cut very thin, and with as little as possible of the white coating between the peel and the fruit.

2. Add sugar, rum and brandy. Stir.

3. Take a ladle full of brandy and light on fire, and ladle gently into bowl. Let it burn for three or four minutes at least, stirring it from time to time. Then extinguish it by covering the basin with a tray, which will immediately put out the flame.

4. Then squeeze in the juice of the three lemons.

5. Add a quart of boiling water. Stir the whole well, cover it up for five minutes, and stir again.

6. Skim off the lemon pieces with a spoon. Take the lemon-peel out, or it will acquire a bitter taste.

7. If not sweet enough, add more sugar to your liking.

8. Serve warm.

NOTE:

The same punch allowed to cool by degrees, and then iced, is delicious. It requires less sugar.

After tea, they had some music. For they were a musical family, and knew what they were about, when they sung a Glee or Catch. . . . Scrooge's niece played well upon the harp; and played among other tunes a simple little air (a mere nothing: you might learn to whistle it in two minutes), which had been familiar to the child who fetched Scrooge from the boarding-school, as he had been reminded by the Ghost of Christmas Past.

*When this strain of music sounded, all the things that
Ghost had shown him, came upon his mind; he softened
more and more. . . .*

Here is another allusion to Fanny and to her children.
Fanny had been sent to music school, and had, after
a time, married another music student, and the two had
moved to Manchester. There she and her husband taught
music, and from time to time, Charles lent or gave them
money. Charles always felt badly that his sister had married badly (in his opinion) and lived so far away. But
there is no question that music introduced throughout
the story is associated with Fanny's family.

Dickens himself was a good singer and liked to sing.
Dickens regarded his comic singing as having saved him
in troubled spots throughout his life. He used it to ingra-
tiate himself with adults and children to good effect as a
youth, and just as much when he was an adult.

*"Forgive me if I am not justified in what I ask," said
Scrooge, looking intently at the Spirit's robe, "but I see
something strange, and not belonging to yourself, pro-
truding from your skirts. Is it a foot or a claw?" . . .*

"Spirit! are they yours?" Scrooge could say no more.

*"They are Man's," said the Spirit, looking down upon
them. "And they cling to me, appealing from their fathers.
This boy is Ignorance. This girl is Want. Beware them*

both, and all of their degree, but most of all beware this
boy, for on his brow I see that written which is Doom,
unless the writing be erased. Deny it!" cried the Spirit,
stretching out its hand towards the city. "Slander those who
tell it ye! Admit it for your factious purposes, and make it
worse. And bide the end!"

For the ending of the second stave, Dickens chose to
close with those who had inspired his tale. These were
the ragged school children, the poor of the city, which he
had seen so many times around London but most ironically near Covent Garden where the storehouses of food
for the city rested.

"Covent-garden Market, when it was market morning,
was wonderful company. The great waggons of cabbages,
with growers' men and boys lying asleep under them, and
with sharp dogs from market-garden neighbourhoods
looking after the whole, were as good as a party. But one
of the worst night sights I know in London, is to be found
in the children who prowl about this place; who sleep
in the baskets, fight for the offal, dart at any object they
think they can lay their thieving hands on, dive under
the carts and barrows, dodge the constables, and are per-
petually making a blunt pattering on the pavement of the
Piazza with the rain of their naked feet. A painful and
unnatural result comes of the comparison one is forced to
institute between the growth of corruption as displayed

in the so much improved and cared for fruits of the earth, and the growth of corruption as displayed in these all uncared for (except inasmuch as ever-hunted) savages," wrote Dickens of Covent Garden.

Of the Ragged Schools, Dickens wrote, "It consisted at that time of either two or three—I forget which—iserable rooms, upstairs in a miserable house. In the best of these, the pupils in the female school were being taught to read and write; and though there were among the number, many wretched creatures steeped in degradation to the lips, they were tolerably quiet, and listened with apparent earnestness and patience to their instructors. The appearance of this room was sad and melancholy, of course—how could it be otherwise!—but, on the whole, encouraging."

Dickens continued, "The close, low chamber at the back, in which the boys were crowded, was so foul and stifling as to be, at first, almost insupportable. But its moral aspect was so far worse than its physical, that this was soon forgotten. Huddled together on a bench about the room, and shown out by some flaring candles stuck against the walls, were a crowd of boys, varying from mere infants to young men; sellers of fruit, herbs, lucifer-matches, flints; sleepers under the dry arches of bridges; young thieves and beggars—with nothing natural to youth about them: with nothing frank, ingenuous, or pleasant in their faces; low-browed, vicious, cunning, wicked; abandoned of all help but this; speeding downward to destruction; and UNUTTERABLY IGNORANT."

". . . [H]e saw before him always the twin phantoms of Ignorance and Want," wrote biographer Peter Ackroyd. "He saw legions of what he called 'Doomed Childhood'. . . ."

"Many of them retire for the night, if they retire at all, under the dry arches of bridges and viaducts; under porticoes; sheds and carts; to outhouses; in sawpits; on staircases," wrote Dickens. In a letter to Angela Burdett-Coutts he had written, "[I have] very seldom seen . . . anything so shocking as the dire neglect of soul and body exhibited in these children . . . in the prodigious misery and ignorance of the swarming masses of mankind in England, the seeds of its certain ruin are sewn."

Dickens harked back, once, to his boot-blacking days, and wrote, in earnest, "I know I do not exaggerate, unconsciously and unintentionally, the scantiness of my resources and the difficulties of my life. I know that if a shilling or so were given to me by anyone I spent it [on] a dinner or tea. I know that I worked from morning to night, with common men and boys. . . . I know that, but for the mercy of God, I might easily have been, for any care that was taken of me, a little robber or a little vagabond."

Stave IV

Ghost of the Future

"Ghost of the Future!" he exclaimed, "I fear you more than any spectre I have seen. But as I know your purpose is to do me good, and as I hope to live to be another man from what I was, I am prepared to bear you company, and do it with a thankful heart. Will you not speak to me?"

It gave him no reply. The hand was pointed straight before them.

Dickens and Forster continued to go back and forth on Dickens' relationship with his publisher. He wrote to Forster on November 19, "I was most horribly put out for a little while; for I had got up early to go at it, and was full of interest in what I had to do. But having eased my mind by that note to you, and taken a turn or two up and down the room, I went at it again, and soon got so interested that I blazed away till 9 last night; only stopping ten minutes for dinner! I suppose I wrote eight printed pages of *Chuzzlewit* yesterday. The consequence is that I could finish to-day, but am taking it easy, and making myself laugh very much."

Returning to *Carol*, with the visitation of this grim ghost, showed Dickens at the height of his literary powers.

The Ghost of Christmas Yet to Come

The Phantom slowly, gravely, silently, approached. When it came near him, Scrooge bent down upon his knee; for in the very air through which this Spirit moved it seemed to scatter gloom and mystery.

It was shrouded in a deep black garment, which concealed its head, its face, its form, and left nothing of it visible save one outstretched hand. But for this it would have been difficult to detach its figure from the night, and separate it from the darkness by which it was surrounded.

here is no question that the Ghost of Christmas Yet to Come is a loosely dressed version of the Angel of Death, a popular character in Western literature. The concept of death as a sentient entity has existed in many societies since the beginning of history. Certainly characters like the Grim Reaper, for example, date back to the fifteenth century. The most popular version was shown as a skeletal figure carrying a large scythe and clothed in a black cloak with a hood.

The Ghost of Christmas Yet to Come, illustrated by John Leech
for the first edition of A Christmas Carol.

Grim Death *by William Strand (1800)*.

The most popular of these was the character "Death" from a popular religious play from the medieval days. "In the play *Everyman*, death is personified and treated as an agent of God that goes to visit the play's protagonist, Everyman. The unknown author of the play uses Death as a character to present a very real truth that all people will meet death. Death is an antagonist in the play and represents physical death," wrote entertainment reporter Daniel Bolton. "The author brings Death into the story to carry out God's will and conviction. Everyman had been living his life according to his own plan and desires. God needed him to realize and see His plan so He calls in Death to carry out His will."

The Exchange

But there they were, in the heart of it; on 'Change, amongst the merchants; who hurried up and down, and chinked the money in their pockets, and conversed in groups, and looked at their watches, and trifled thoughtfully with their great gold seals; and so forth, as Scrooge had seen them often.

The first place the Ghost of Christmas Yet to Come brings Scrooge is the Exchange. Bankers and businessmen who owned counting houses bought and sold lists of debtors in the halls and steps of the Royal Stock Exchange. They destroyed many lives in doing so.

Charles Dickens Jr. wrote, "[The] Royal Exchange was opened by Queen Victoria on January 1st, 1845. It was

built after the designs of Sir W. Tite, and cost no less
than £150,000. The old Exchange, which occupied the
present site, was built after the Great Fire, and again suffered from the same element in 1838. The first Exchange
was opened by Queen Elizabeth in 1570, who, by her
herald, declared the house to be 'The Royal Exchange.'
Sir Thomas Gresham introduced exchanges into England,
but they had been popular in most of the commercial
cities of Italy, Germany, and the Netherlands, many years
previous to their adoption in England."

Dickens loathed the Royal Exchange, as seen in
his diary entry from January 10, 1838, when he wrote,
"At work all day and to a quadrille party at night. City
people and rather dull. Intensely cold coming home, and
vague reports of a fire somewhere. Frederick [mentions]
the Royal Exchange, at which I sneer most sagely. . . ."
The next day he wrote, "To-day the papers are full of it,
and it was the Royal Exchange. . . . Called on Browne
and went with him to see the ruins, of which we saw
much as we should have done if we had stopped home."
Despite his dislike of what the Exchange stood for, it was
a popular milestone in his nightly walks and was surely on
his mind and inspired some part of his story.

The Pawnbroker

Scrooge and the Phantom came into the presence of this man, just as a woman with a heavy bundle slunk into the shop. But she had scarcely entered, when another woman, similarly laden, came in too; and she was closely followed by a man in faded black, who was no less startled by the sight of them, than they had been upon the recognition of each other.

Now Dickens dove deep into his past, and went to a part of his own life that had been so painful he could not bear it. He must have wandered one of these nights up Hampstead Road to revisit the scene of this personal ghost to refresh his mind of the details. But the reality of it must have been overwhelming.

After his father had been placed in Marshalsea, but before his mother joined her husband, there was a period when Elizabeth Dickens attempted to keep her family and her house together. But with mounting bills and no credit, it was hard to take care of and feed the growing Dickens family.

Elizabeth attempted to open a school, spending many hours and a little money they could not spare to open her own little business at Bayham Street named "Mrs. Dickens Establishment." As Dickens later remembered, ". . . nobody ever came to the school, nor do I recollect that anybody ever proposed to come, or that the least preparation was made to receive anybody." The scheme came to nothing. The wolf was at the door.

". . . [H]is distracted mother tried to keep things going and the whimpering children fed by pawning brooches and spoons and gradually stripping the rooms bare of furniture. Charles became well known to the pawnbroker's shop, where the broker or his principal clerk, while making out the pawn ticket, would often hear him conjugate a Latin verb or decline *musa* and *dominus*," wrote Edgar Johnson of Dickens.

"Charles, as the man of the family, just twelve years old, was sent to a pawnbroker in the Hampstead Road, first with the books that he loved, then with items of furniture, until after a few weeks the house was almost empty, and the family was camping out in two bare rooms in the cold weather," wrote Claire Tomalin.

Awful memories to conjure on a cold night's walk on the dark streets of London. The sugar tongs and sheets and clothes that Scrooge saw the charwoman and undertaker flipping through in the pawnshop were in reality the property of John and Elizabeth Dickens then, via the courier of a child. To see strangers fumble through the things of one's life, hoping for money to feed your family—these were not memories that kept one warm. Surely these memories must have brought tears to Mr. Dickens' eyes.

The Death of Tiny Tim

"Yes, my dear," returned Bob. "I wish you could have gone. It would have done you good to see how green a place it is But you'll see it often. I promised him that I would walk there on a Sunday. My little, little child!" cried Bob. "My little child!"

If Tiny Tim had died, as the Ghost of Christmas Yet to Come suggested he might if things did not change, it would have been most likely from tuberculosis. The symptoms included flushed cheeks, bright eyes, fever, loss of appetite, and most of all, a persistent cough.

It was a very common ailment of the Victorian era, most commonly called "consumption" on both sides of the Atlantic. Victorian scholar Constance Manoli-Skocay wrote, "It was feared, but regarded with a peculiar resignation because it was so unavoidable. It was dreaded, but at the same time romanticized. It was a disease that reflected the culture of its time: the victim slowly, gracefully fading away, transcending their corporeal body, their immortal soul shining through. . . . It affected the poor more often than the wealthy, females more than males, and people of all ages. Anyone could be a victim, but it was especially prevalent among young adults, cruelly striking down those in the prime of their lives." The end came slowly, and painfully, for the victim as well as for the survivors.

In his lifetime, Charles Dickens had known the death of a child. His little sister Harriet had died in the year the family moved to Bayham Street. Harriet Dickens had been born in 1819 and died in 1824. It is not recorded whether she died in Chatham or on Bayham Street, but surely the memories must have been vivid as Charles was twelve years old at the time. One can almost see the stricken John and Elizabeth Dickens smote with grief, as were Bob and Martha Cratchit at the prospect of their son's demise. So as the Cratchits were at Christmas, one may assume that this too was taken from Dickens family's memories.

The Graveyard

"Before I draw nearer to that stone to which you point,"
said Scrooge, "answer me one question. Are these the
shadows of the things that Will be, or are they shadows of
things that May be, only?"

How ironic that the last scene with the Ghost of Christmas Yet to Come should occur where Dickens started so long ago. Possibly four or five weeks after he began, here we are back in the graveyard where Dickens had first found his main character not two or three years earlier.

Certainly, in Victorian England, cemeteries had in some respects become the metropolis of the dead. And the hierarchy of society had imposed itself even on the world of the deceased. In some instances, the best cemeteries were like parks. Londoners were forced to deal with this problem of what to do with the dead in a growing city like London during the industrial age, when more folks from the farmlands were coming to the cities for jobs and to enjoy the spoils of a mechanized society. In 1832, Parliament passed a law that closed the inner-city London churchyards to new internments. Following that law, new cemeteries were established between 1832 (Kensal Green) and 1841 (Tower Hamlets). The most famous of these was Highgate Cemetery in 1839.

There is no question that Ebenezer Scroggie's headstone—labeled "mean man" as far as Dickens was concerned (instead of what it actually said, "meal man")—is where the story really began, and where it needs to end for the purposes of the main character's personal journey.

That Scroggie's tombstone is now lost to history can be seen, at least ironically, as Scrooge's fate had not the spirits showed him a better path. Since Dickens wrote *A Christmas Carol*, innumerable stories have adapted similar endings, the most noteworthy being Frank Capra's colorful retelling of *A Christmas Carol* (in a sense) as *It's A Wonderful Life*, as film critic Roger Ebert noted, "a sort of *Christmas Carol* in reverse." Capra's climactic moment comes when Clarence, an angel, shows George Baily the grave of his brother rather than his own.

As in the medieval tale *Everyman*, Scrooge, like all men (and women), must face his transition from this life, and must count what his or her life has meant. What has each of us left behind? Other than our own wants and desires, what have we done for the benefit of our fellow man? This concept of legacy and charity are two of the main themes that Dickens wrote about in his novella that have given many readers serious pause, which is what Dickens was hoping for in the first place.

Stave V

Redemption

"I will live in the Past, the Present, and the Future!"
Scrooge repeated, as he scrambled out of bed. "The Spirits
of all Three shall strive within me. Oh Jacob Marley!
Heaven, and the Christmas Time be praised for this! I say
it on my knees, old Jacob; on my knees!"

The redemption of Scrooge has, without a doubt, pleased more people than almost any other character development Dickens had ever created. And it has been written about by scholars since its first publication. But what is it about Scrooge's reclamation that draws us so?

"Marley's Ghost is the symbol of divine grace, and the three Christmas Spirits are the working of that grace through the agencies of memory, example, and fear. And Scrooge, although of course he is himself too, is himself not alone: he is the embodiment of all that concentration upon material power and callous indifference to the welfare of human beings that the economists had erected into a system, businessmen and industrialists pursued relentlessly, and society had taken for granted as inevitable and proper. The conversion of Scrooge is an image of the conversion for which Dickens hopes among mankind," wrote Edgar Johnson.

"In *A Christmas Carol* Dickens imagines what he once was and what he might have become . . . he wanted to recreate the atmosphere of the fairy stories which he had read as a child; but one in which he was the real hero too," wrote Peter Ackroyd.

> *"An intelligent boy!" said Scrooge. "A remarkable boy! Do you know whether they've sold the prize Turkey that was hanging up there?—Not the little prize Turkey: the big one?"*
>
> *"What, the one as big as me?" returned the boy.*
>
> *"What a delightful boy!" said Scrooge. "It's a pleasure to talk to him. Yes, my buck!"*
>
> *"It's hanging there now," replied the boy.*
>
> *"Is it?" said Scrooge. "Go and buy it."*

Surely, Dickens did not invent the Christmas goose or turkey. Washington Irving had written about it years before, in a book Dickens knew well, entitled, *Old Christmas*, which related time he had spent in an old English castle, Aston Hall, on holiday season in 1820.

"Perhaps the impending holiday might have given a more than usual animation to the country, for it seemed to me as if everybody was in good looks and good spirits. Game, poultry, and other luxuries of the table were in brisk circulation in the villages; the grocers', butchers', and fruiterers' shops were thronged with customers. The housewives were stirring briskly about, putting their dwellings in order, and the glossy branches of holly, with their bright red berries, began to appear at the windows. The scene brought to mind an old writer's account of Christmas preparation: 'Now capons and hens, besides turkeys, geese, and ducks, with beef and mutton—must all die; for in twelve days a multitude of people will not be fed with a little. Now plums and spice, sugar and honey, square it among pies and broth. Now or never must music be in tune, for the youth must dance and sing to get them a heat, while the aged sit by the fire. The country maid leaves half her market, and must be sent again, if she forgets a pack of cards on Christmas Eve. Great is the contention of Holly and Ivy, whether master or dame wears the breeches. Dice and cards benefit the butler; and if the cook do not lack wit, he will sweetly lick his fingers,' " wrote Irving.

But one question continued to vex some folks—was it a goose or a turkey that Scrooge should have bought?

"In fact, as everyone surely knew, Turkey was a North American fowl. Scrooge buying a turkey instead of a goose in London Town would be as improbable as a London clubman ordering bourbon and ginger ale instead of Scotch and soda," wrote popular columnist Russell Baker.

However turkey was not unknown to Londoners by the mid-1800s. Turkey was most commonly referred to as "Indian chicken," much like corn was called "Indian corn," etc. Even the French referred to it as coq d'Inde. In Austria turkeys in common parlance were called simply "Indians."

Turkey had been in Europe for some time. Most modern domesticated turkey is descended from one of six subspecies of wild turkey found in present day Mexico. Domestic turkeys were taken to Europe by the Spanish, which evolved into current popular breeds as Spanish Black and the Royal Palm. It is widely credited that the sixteenth-century English navigator William Strickland introduced the bird to the British Isles. English farmer Thomas Tusser noted the turkey being among farmers' fare at Christmas in 1573. Prior to the late nineteenth century, turkey was something of a luxury in the United Kingdom, with goose or beef a more common Christmas dinner among the working classes.

There is no question, too, that Dickens had just returned from America, where turkey was a common meal, and was served especially on festive occasions. Dickens must surely have partaken of turkey during his stay, thus it found its way into the story.

Popular cookbooks of the time also call for turkey and goose. Here is how Mrs. Beeton, the most popular English cookbook author of the mid-nineteenth century, writes about the Christmas turkey in *Mrs. Beeton's Every Day Cookery and Housekeeping Book*:

"A noble dish is a turkey, roast or boiled. A Christmas dinner, with the middle-class of this empire, would scarcely be a Christmas dinner without its turkey; and we can hardly imagine an object of greater envy than that presented by a respected portly paterfamilias carving, at the season devoted to good cheer and genial charity, his own fat turkey, and carving it well."

"So, the turkey that Scrooge purchased—the huge bird that could 'never could have stood upon his legs'—was a prize bird that hung in the poulterer's window to draw people in. It wasn't the only prize bird—there were two prize birds in the window—a little one and a big one. The prize birds were everyone's dream, but they couldn't afford to eat these dreams—on Christmas Day these visions of unlimited bounty were still unsold. What people actually served at home for the Christmas dinner were smaller turkeys—very likely the eight to twelve pounds implied by Mrs. Beeton's recipe," wrote William Rubel, a food historian.

The Solicitor Redux

"Mr. Scrooge?"

"Yes," said Scrooge. "That is my name, and I fear it may not be pleasant to you. Allow me to ask your pardon. And will you have the goodness"—here Scrooge whispered in his ear.

"Lord bless me!" cried the gentleman, as if his breath were taken away. "My dear Mr. Scrooge, are you serious?"

"If you please," said Scrooge. "Not a farthing less. A great many back-payments are included in it, I assure you. Will you do me that favour?"

As Scrooge made his way upon the streets of the Old City, he happened to bump into the portlier of the two gentlemen who had just visited him the previous morning asking for donations to the poor. Though we never know the amount, Scrooge is clearly incredibly generous, and his reclamation takes one more step forward.

Of course, Dickens himself did much for charity in his life. He was often called upon to perform at benefits which would raise money for various and sundry causes. Dickens may not have had an overarching vision of how to reform society, but he was a philanthropist.

He worked for more than a decade to establish a project to help destitute girls and young women in mid-nineteenth century London. Urania Cottage was a safe house for young women in Shepherd's Bush, saving young women from lives of prostitution and crime. He supported his brother-in-law's Health of Towns Association, pressing for reform of housing and sanitation of the poor. And he was adamant in helping the Children Hospital to insure proper medical care for the poorest children of London.

"The truth is that Dickens's criticism of society is almost exclusively moral. Hence the utter lack of any constructive suggestion anywhere in his work," wrote George Orwell. "For in reality his target is not so much society as 'human nature.'"

Christmas with Fred

"Why bless my soul!" cried Fred, "who's that?"
"It's I. Your uncle Scrooge. I have come to dinner. Will
you let me in, Fred?"

What strikes the reader immediately is the familial bond which Scrooge calls upon ("Uncle") to signal his contrition to Fred. After the previous day's meeting, Fred immediately picks up on the reference and signals his willingness to entertain his uncle.

Family was important to Dickens. And he knew it was just as important to his readers, and to the story. As Mamie Dickens later recalled, "On Christmas Day we all had our glasses filled, and then my father, raising his, would say: 'Here's to us all. God bless us!' a toast which was rapidly and willingly drunk. His conversation, as may be imagined, was often extremely humorous, and I have seen the servants, who were waiting at table, convulsed often with laughter at his droll remarks and stories. Now, as I recall these gatherings, my sight grows blurred with the tears that rise to my eyes. But I love to remember them, and to see, if only in memory, my father at his own table, surrounded by his own family and friends— a beautiful Christmas spirit."

Frederick Dickens.

Also, this scene, real or imagined, was a symbolic gesture then to his brother Fred, with whom he was slowly becoming estranged. This was symbolic of his own personal life, painful as it was, that he would not see his own brother at Christmas.

Bob Cratchit's Raise

"A merry Christmas, Bob!" said Scrooge, with an earnestness that could not be mistaken, as he clapped him on the back. "A merrier Christmas, Bob, my good fellow, than I have given you, for many a year! I'll raise your salary, and endeavour to assist your struggling family, and we will discuss your affairs this very afternoon, over a Christmas bowl of smoking bishop, Bob! Make up the fires, and buy another coal-scuttle before you dot another i, Bob Cratchit!"

The final act of Scrooge's reclamation is to repair his relationship with Bob Cratchit. He waits for Cratchit, arriving at his office early the next day, and ambushes the clerk when he arrives late. But it's all farce, as Scrooge offers Cratchit a raise and offers to help him with Tiny Tim as well.

Even today, there are defenders of Scrooge's pre-reclamation ways who cry "Ba! Humbug!" at Scrooge's change of heart.

Yaron Brook, president and executive director of the Ayn Rand Institute, defended Scrooge's miserly treatment of his beleaguered clerk. Brook said Cratchit was getting paid the market wage and that his boss had no moral obligation to help him out.

"I assume if somebody else was willing to pay him more, that he would move jobs and no one would feel sorry for Scrooge if [Cratchit] just walked up and left because he got more money somewhere else," Brook said. "If he's making very little, it's probably because he adds very little productive value to the economy, to business. That's the reality of the market place and there's nothing unjust about that." To their insistence, those who still champion the unredeemed Scrooge point out that Cratchit was paid fifteen shillings a week, about average for a clerk and double what a general laborer earned.

In fact, Scrooge's decision at the end of the story to boost Cratchit's salary would be a "disastrous course of action in real life," Brook said, adding that Scrooge's clients would suffer because he has less money to reinvest into lending *them* money.

Jim Lacey, author and analyst at the Institute for
Defense Analyses, bemoaned Scrooge's turn to altruism,
saying it was unfortunate for the "many thousands whose
jobs Scrooge's investments had underwritten" as his
"transfer of funds to less productive causes undoubtedly
cost them dearly."

Still, the working class understood the heroism it took
for Scrooge to help out a fellow human being who was
absolutely in need. And deep in the recesses of his mind,
hadn't he wished as a child that someone would have
done the same for his father? This must have been a deep-
seated issue in the mind of the author, a reworking of his
life into a fairytale ending.

Long Live Tiny Tim

Scrooge was better than his word. He did it all, and infinitely more; and to Tiny Tim, who did NOT die, he was a second father. He became as good a friend, as good a master, and as good a man, as the good old city knew, or any other good old city, town, or borough, in the good old world.

If rickets and malnutrition were the only culprits, Scrooge's intervention might not have been enough. The fact that tuberculosis (TB) might have been part of Tim's diagnosis might have proved more problematic for Tim. The scientific community hadn't really come to terms with TB's being contagious. The sanatorium movement began in the late 1800s to segregate infected patients out of the main stream, as well as identifying it being a viral infection. The first successful cure was produced in 1906 in France. The current course of treatment requires a long series of strict drug programs which in modern times may take six to twelve months.

Both rickets and TB can be improved and indeed cured through increased exposure to Vitamin D, which can be obtained through exposure to sunlight and a balanced diet.

As the Ghost of Christmas Present showed Ebenezer Scrooge, Tiny Tim's condition would be fatal without a different course for the boy. According to Dr. Chesney's research, Scrooge could have ensured several areas were covered to help Tiny Tim simply through his improved generosity to Bob Cratchit and his family.

"How could Scrooge, who upon his transformation embraced being Tiny Tim's 'second father,' have had such an effect as to save Tim? He could have ensured that Tim received a better diet, including fish, dairy products, good quality bread, and more calories. Trips to the countryside would have increased sunshine exposure. Medical specialists could have advised more contemporary and possibly effective orthopedic devices, and, with the curing of rickets, Tim's limbs may have become straighter," wrote Dr. Chesney. "We are not told whether he was fully cured, but he definitely survived."

He had no further intercourse with Spirits, but lived upon the Total Abstinence Principle, ever afterwards; and it was always said of him, that he knew how to keep Christmas well, if any man alive possessed the knowledge. May that be truly said of us, and all of us! And so, as Tiny Tim observed,

God bless Us, Every One!

Dickens Cuts Loose

t was the very beginning of December. He had finished writing the book in just six weeks.

Once the manuscript for *A Christmas Carol* was finished, Dickens prepared the book for publication. During the course of writing, Dickens had made hundreds of corrections, scribbles, and cross outs. He had to make sure these all came through properly in the final pages.

Since the book was being distributed by Chapman and Hall, with Dickens producing it, he fiddled constantly with the package. He put a laser focus on the final details. The exterior featured a red case with gold gilt embossing and with the title and Dickens' name encircled by a wreath of holly, and the edges of the pages were covered in gold gilt. Inside, the endpapers were colored and there were eight illustrative plates throughout. He had spared no expense, so that the book might be as pleasant a property, and might seem as small and gifty as possible. And to make sure the book would fly out of the stores he put the low price of five shillings on it, ensuring its success.

In this new scheme, Dickens was all but assured that if it were a success, he would enjoy the resulting monies all the more. He had borrowed money against it, so sure was he of the book's power and attractiveness.

Just before publication he received a letter from John Leech, the illustrator, who had drawn the eight art pieces in the book. Leech was unhappy with the color plates, which were hand tinted. Phiz's son, Edgar Browne, later wrote, "This was a primitive process. Leech of course set the pattern, the copyist would spread out a number of print all around a large table, having a number of saucers ready prepared with the appropriate tints . . . and then would start off and tint all the skies, then all the coats, and so on, till every object was separately colored, and the work was done. The effect was certainly gay, but general too crude to be pleasant."

Dickens responded to Leech's complaints on December 14, 1843, writing, "I do not doubt, in my own mind, that you unconsciously exaggerate the evil done by the colorers. You can't think how much better they will look in a neat book, than you suppose. But I have sent a Strong Dispatch to C[hapman] and H[all], and will report to you when I hear from them. I quite agree with you, that it is a point of great importance."

The book was published on December 19, 1843. And then Dickens dove into the Christmas season.

"At Christmas 1843 Dickens, for all his pressing problems, managed to maintain a high level of seasonal jollity. Macready was away acting in America, and Dickens and Forster appointed themselves chief entertainers at the children's party given by Mrs. Macready on Boxing Day," wrote Claire Tomalin.

Catherine Macready was the wife of the famed English actor William Charles Macready, who that season was away in the United States on tour.

Jane Carlyle later related on the occasion, "Dickens and Forster above all exerted themselves till the perspiration was pouring down and they seemed drunk with their efforts. Only think of the excellent D[ickens] playing the conjuror for a whole hour—the best conjuror I ever saw—(and I have paid money to see several)— and Forster acting as his servant. This part of the entertainment concluded with a plum pudding made out of raw flour, raw eggs—all the usual ingredients—boiled in a gentleman's hat—and tumbled out reeking—all in one minute before the eyes of the astonished children and astonished grown people." She also relayed how fun it was to watch the adults all swinging about, dancing, even the "gigantic Thackeray."

After Macready's event, Dickens convinced William Makepeace Thackeray and John Forster to come back to Devonshire Terrace where they ended the night with drinks all around.

In a letter to Prof. Cornelius Felton in Cambridge, Massachusetts, Dickens excitedly told of how he celebrated to all ends, writing, "Forster is out again; and if he don't go in again, after the manner in which we have been keeping Christmas, he must be very strong indeed. Such dinings, such dancings, such conjurings, such blindman's-bluffings, such theater goings, such kissings-out of the old years and kissings-in of the new ones, never took place in these parts before. To keep the *Chuzzlewit* going, and this little book, the *Carol*, in the odd times between the parts of it, was, as you may suppose, pretty tight work. But when it was done I broke out like a mad man. And if you could have seen me at the Children's party at the Macready's the other night, going down a country dance with Mrs. M., you would have thought I was a country gentleman of independent property, residing on a tip top farm, with the wind blowing straight in my face the other day."

"Good God, how we missed you," Dickens wrote to William Charles Macready who was touring in America, "talked of you, drank to your health, and wondered what you were doing! Perhaps you . . . feel a little sore—just a little bit, you know, the merest trifle in the world—on hearing that Mrs. Macready looked brilliant, blooming,

young, and handsome, and that she danced a country
dance with the writer hereof. . . . Now you don't like to
be told that? Nor do you like to hear that Forster and I
conjured bravely, that a plum pudding was produced from
an empty saucepan, held over a blazing fire kindled in
Stanfield's hat without damage to the lining; that a box
of brand was changed into a live guinea-pig, which ran
between your godchild's feet, and was the cause of such a
shrill uproar and clapping of hands that you might have
heard it (and I daresay did) in America. . . ."

Success!

The book was published December 19, 1843. The first printing of 6,000 copies sold out in the first week! A huge number by today's standards, but even more impressive back then. Six more reprintings, in much smaller numbers, totaled to approximately 7,000 additional copies. The book was the success Dickens had hoped it would be.

"Never had little book an outset so full of brilliancy of promise. Published but a few days before Christmas, it was hailed on every side with enthusiastic greeting. The first edition of six thousand copies was sold the first day," wrote Forster. "What was marked in him to the last was manifest now. He had identified himself with Christmas fancies. Its life and spirits, its humor in riotous abundance, of right belonged to him. Its imaginations as well as kindly thoughts were his; and its privilege to light up with some sort of comfort the squalidest places, he had made his own. Christmas Day was not more social or welcome: New Year's Day not more new: Twelfth Night not more full of characters. The duty of diffusing enjoyment had never been taught by a more abundant, mirthful, thoughtful, ever-seasonable writer."

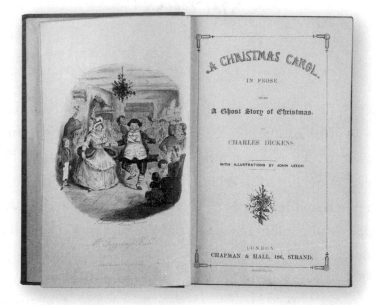

Title page to the 1843 first edition of A Christmas Carol.

"The book went straight to the heart of the public and has remained lodged there ever since, with its mixture of horror, despair, hope and warmth, its message— a Christmas message—that even the worst of sinners may repent and become a good man; and its insistence that good cheer, food and drink shared, gifts and even dancing are not merely frivolous pleasures but basic expressions of love and mutual support among all human beings," wrote Claire Tomalin.

Thomas Carlyle, the Scottish historian (whom Dickens greatly admired), went straight out and bought himself a turkey after reading A *Christmas Carol* and ate it.

Dickens' literary rival and friend William Makepeace Thackeray exclaimed, "Who can listen to objections regarding such a book as this? It seems to me a national benefit, and to every man or woman who reads it a personal kindness."

Fellow novelist Margaret Oliphant said that although it was "the apotheosis of turkey and plum pudding, [it] moved us all in those days as if it had been a new gospel."

The most interesting comments on the book came from Henry Wadsworth Longfellow's wife, Frances, who was enthusiastic about *Carol*. She and Longfellow read it together after midnight on January 27, 1844, and she presumably spoke for both when she called it "an admirable performance with a true Christmas glow about it, yet very pathetic and poetical besides." A few days later, in a separate letter, she wrote, "Have you seen Dickens' 'Christmas Carol'? He sent it to Felton in its English garb, with capital woodcuts, and a nice clear type! It is a most admirable production I think, and has had great success in England, comforting people for the tediousness of *Chuzzlewit*. It is evidently written at heart and from the heart, and has a Christmas crackle and glow about it, besides much pathos and poetry of conception, which form a rich combination. The sketch of the poor clerk's dinner is in his best manner, and almost consoles one for the poverty it reveals."

Mrs. Longfellow's opinion was a popular one. The public agreed. Whereas his long absence in America, and the disaster of *Chuzzlewit*, had dampened his reputation, *A Christmas Carol* immediately reestablished Dickens as one of the most popular and literate writers in the world. It absolutely saved his reputation.

"He was one of the oddest men to ever take up a pen. And yet this egregious figure, this uncommon man, held a position in the hearts and minds of his readers, especially the working man and woman, like no other. He seemed to be writing for them, on their behalf, voicing their hopes and beliefs, celebrating their lives. And in none of his works did he do this more than in *A Christmas Carol*, the book in which, if he didn't actually invent it, he permanently transformed the meaning of Christmas," wrote actor and scholar Simon Callow.

Peter Ackroyd made a bolder case, writing, "Christmas cards were not introduced until 1846, and Christmas crackers until the 1850s. Typically it was still a one-day holiday when presents were given to children, but there was no orgy of benevolence and generosity. It was a time of quiet rest. Acting. Reading aloud. Music. Games. What Dickens did was to transform the holiday by suffusing it with his own particular mixture of aspirations, memories, and fears." But Ackroyd also went on to say, "Dickens had an acute sense of, a need for, 'Home'—it sprang from his own experience of being banished from that blessed place—which is why in A Christmas Carol . . . there is a constant contrast between warmth and cold, between the rich and the poor, between the well and the ill, between the need for comfort and the anxiety of homelessness. "

"Dickens, with his A Christmas Carol, more than any other person helped to shape and invent the modern Christmas," wrote Christmas historian Mark Connelly. "But surely one of the reasons for the success of Dickens was that people understood and related to the tale."

Disappointment . . .

Within two weeks of the publication of A *Christmas Carol*, pirated editions were already on the stands. These "condensations" were little more than slight rewrites at best. Many had flat-out pirated the text. This was an ongoing situation for Dickens for most of his literary career, but soon after the book was published, he spent time and money fighting off these editions.

On January 6, 1844, Dickens instructed his lawyer Mitton, with whom he had shared that train ride so seemingly long ago, to institute chancery proceedings against Parley's Penny Library. They had published *A Christmas Ghost Story Reoriginated from the Original by Charles Dickens*. Dickens soon found himself in a "world of injunctions, motions for dissolution, affidavits, vice-chancellors, and other intricate and costly legalities."

Dickens was so obsessed and mortified he even attended one of the innumerable unauthorized dramatizations of his play being performed throughout London. "I saw the Carol last night," he wrote to Forster of a dramatic performance at the Adelphi. "Better than usual, and Wright seems to enjoy Bob Cratchit, but heart-breaking to me. Oh Heaven! if any forecast of this was ever in my mind! Yet O. Smith was drearily better than I expected."

But more bad news was on the doorstep. When the accountings for A Christmas Carol arrived, Dickens was horrified.

He had hoped to earn a £1,000 from the sale of the book, but the production costs—the tinted illustrations, the fancy endpapers, the gilding, etc.—had cut heavily into the profits.

"The first six thousand copies show a profit of 230 pounds!" he wrote to Forster. It was actually much less in retrospect.

Forster wrote in his biography of Dickens, "It may interest the reader, and be something of a curiosity of literature, if I give the expenses of the first edition of 6000, and of the 7000 more which constituted the five following editions, with the profit of the remaining 2000 which completed the sale of fifteen thousand." The tables that follow are faithfully reproduced from Forster's original writings.

CHRISTMAS CAROL.
1st Edition, 6000 No.

1843
Dec.

	£	_s._	_d._
Printing	74	2	9
Paper	89	2	0
Drawings and Engravings	49	18	0
Two Steel Plates	1	4	0
Printing Plates	15	17	6
Paper for do	7	12	0
Colouring Plates	120	0	0
Binding	180	0	0
Incidents and Advertising	168	7	8
Commission	99	4	6
	£805	8	5

2nd to the 7th Edition, making 7000 Copies.

1844.
Jan.

	£	_s._	_d._
Printing	58	18	0
Paper	103	19	0
Printing Plates	17	10	0
Paper	8	17	4
Colouring Plates	140	0	0
Binding	199	18	2
Incidents and Advertising	83	5	8
Commission	107	18	10
	£720	7	0

"Two thousand more, represented by the last item in the subjoined balance, were sold before the close of the year, leaving a remainder of seventy copies."

1843			£	_s._	_d._
Dec. Balance of a/c to			186	16	7
Mr. Dickens's credit					
1844					
Jan. to April.	Do.	Do.	349	12	0
May to Dec.	Do.	Do.	189	11	5
Amount of Profit on the Work			£726	0	0

"But this is a chapter of disappointments," Forster wrote. While Dickens had begrudgingly accepted *Chuzzlewit's* lukewarm reception, which seemed "distant and problematical, so even the prodigious immediate success of the *Christmas Carol* itself was not to be an unmitigated pleasure."

On January 10, 1844, Dickens wrote to Forster, "Such a night as I have passed! I really believed I should never get up again, until I had passed through all the horrors of a fever. I found the *Carol* accounts awaiting me, and they were the cause of it. The first six thousand copies show a profit of £230! And the last four will yield as much more. I had set my heart and soul upon a Thousand, clear. What a wonderful thing it is, that such a great success should occasion me such intolerable anxiety and disappointment!"

Dickens would go on to complain that Chapman and Hall had not properly advertised the book, and that they had layered in numerous charges to his accounting. Still, the sales of the book had been spectacular in such a short burst. Ironically, in December 1844, he would publish *The Chimes*, one of his several other Christmas writings, which sold fewer copies but netted him more than £1,500—much more than *Carol*.

"My year's bills, unpaid, are so terrific," Dickens wrote, "that all the energy and determination I can possibly exert will be required to clear me before I go abroad; which, if next June come and find me alive, I shall do. Good Heaven, if I had only taken heart a year ago! Do come soon, as I am very anxious to talk with you. We can send round to Mac after you arrive, and tell him to join us at Hampstead or elsewhere. I was so utterly knocked down last night, that I came up to the contemplation of all these things quite bold this morning. If I can let the house for this season, I will be off to some seaside place as soon as a tenant offers. I am not afraid, if I reduce my expenses; but if I do not, I shall be ruined past all mortal hope of redemption."

"And indeed this was his panic and fear: the fear of ruin, of being thrust down again into poverty, to go the way of his father into a debtors' prison, all the success and fame he has achieved to be stripped from him as he is cast back into the state of childhood," wrote Ackroyd with keen insight. "There must have been times when it seemed to him that all his achievement was a dream, and that he would wake up once again in Bayham Street or the little attic room of Lant Street. There was still so much fear behind the bright appearance of the eminent novelist."

But Dickens was not done tinkering with A *Christmas Carol*. No, the tinkering had just begun.

The First Reading

Christmas Carol had performed a miracle in Dickens' present career, and it was still to have immense influence on him the rest of his life—especially his public life. He was now about to ascend from a literary star to a performing one, which would enhance his public persona and reputation in a much bigger way.

In January 1853, Dickens visited Birmingham, probably having taken the first leg of the same train he had taken on his way to Manchester in 1843. He had arrived there to receive a diamond ring and other presents from the city's Society of Artists. Dickens already owned a diamond ring, but replaced it with the gift to show his appreciation. Following the presentation there was a banquet in this honor.

While at that event he came to find out about the founding of a new industrial and literary institute in the city. The Birmingham and Midland Institute, now on Margaret Street in the city center of Birmingham, was a pioneer of adult scientific and technical education and also offered arts and science lectures, exhibitions, and concerts. The idea was to make education available to working people. Of course, this was something that immediately appealed to Dickens and could not but help bring back memories of events a decade earlier in Manchester. The idea of bringing education to the masses was always delightful news to him.

During the ceremony, Dickens had voiced his disbelief in "the coxcombical idea of writing down to the popular intelligence," and his belief in the populace. In his view, the working class "had set literature free." Dickens also said in that same speech, "I believe no true man, with anything to tell, need have the least misgiving, either for himself or for his message, before a large number of hearers."

"On the way to the railway station after the banquet, it suddenly occurred to him that he could help raise money for the venture by giving a public reading in Birmingham," wrote Ackroyd.

Arriving home in London, Dickens, who was then working on *Bleak House*, wrote to one of the founders of the Institute, "there would be some novelty in the thing, as I have never done it in public, though I have in private and (if I may say so) with a great effect on the hearers." Dickens suggested he perform in December of that year. Dickens' only stipulation was that "working people" should be let in free to sit beside the middle classes. The Society agreed after some negotiations, and a date was set during the Christmas season of that same year. He had consented to read the *Carol* on the 27th and *The Cricket on the Hearth* on the 29th.

Dickens had read *A Christmas Carol* to a group of English friends who were living in Italy in 1844, the same year he and his family lived there. Dickens had attempted to cancel this private engagement when he learned that the hosts had invited "strangers" to hear him. Once the dispute was settled, Dickens visited and nervously read the story to them. One of the guests remembered years later that Dickens was very nervous and refused to have anyone sit behind him during the length of the reading. He wanted everyone to be in front of him, where he could see them, and where they could be under the gaze of his magnetic eyes.

Months passed and December finally rolled around. By mid-month, he was well into preparing for his reading. His wife, Catherine, and her sister Georgina (Georgy) accompanied him to Birmingham with several of their older children. The Birmingham Town Hall was an enormous building, and this was no small affair. Birmingham

Town Hall remains a highly rated concert hall and venue for popular assemblies, opened in 1834 in Victoria Square. The first of the monumental town halls that would come to characterize the cities of Victorian England, Birmingham Town Hall was also the first significant work of the nineteenth-century revival of Roman architecture. The design was based on the proportions of the Temple of Castor and Pollux in the Roman Forum. With its large, triangular, plain façade sitting atop eight giant columns, this white structure dominated Birmingham's cityscape at the time.

Birmingham Town Hall.

On December 27 there was a snowstorm in Birmingham. Wind whipped through the city's streets with blinding swirls of snow and sleet. The hall was packed with somewhere between 1,700 and 2,000 people, and "the enthusiasm was great," according to Forster.

"As a child Charles was exposed to, and loved, the theater. As a schoolboy he formed a small dramatic company of his friends," wrote Dickens historian David Perdue. "Had it not been for an illness on the morning of a scheduled audition at the Covent Garden Theater in the early 1830s, just before his writing gained attention, he may have made a career on the stage." Now here he was in Birmingham.

On December 27, 1853, Charles Dickens ascended the stage for the first time to give a dramatic reading of *A Christmas Carol* in front of a paying crowd. He had spoken publicly before, mostly giving speeches, but he had never read from one of his books. In fact, up to that time no major novelist had ever read from one of their works for the public in such a way. He was about to make history.

Dickens, dressed impeccably, walked up to the stage nervously. A rousing applause filled the massive hall. He looked over the assembled group, which he knew had travelled through rough weather just to see him. The venue was magnitudes larger than the Manchester Athenaeum. It was understandable that he should feel uncomfortable in such an unusual situation.

"I had not considered all that carefully, and I believe made the most distant person hear as well as if I had been reading in my own room," he later admitted.

Once he was positioned on stage and din of the audience had reduced to a hush, Dickens began.

"Marely was dead. . . ."

The crowd became silent as the well-dressed yet nervous author quickly took command. The performance lasted three hours, though he originally predicted it would be two. And he forgot his nerves a little way into the reading, later telling a friend, ". . . we were all going on together, in the first page, so easily, to all appearance, as if we had been sitting around the fire."

"Dickens's delighted enjoyment, in fact, of everything in any way connected with the theatrical profession, was second only to that shown by him in the indulgence of the master-passion of his life, his love of literature. The way in which he threw himself into his labors, as a Reader, was only another indication of his intense affection for the dramatic art. For, as we have already insisted, the Readings were more than simply Readings, they were in the fullest meaning of the words singularly ingenious and highly elaborated histrionic performances. And his sustained success in them during fifteen years altogether, and, as we have seen, through as many as five hundred representations, may be accounted for in the same way as his still more prolonged success, from the beginning of his career as a Novelist down to its very close . . . as the most popular author of his generation," remembered Charles Kent of Dickens' talents. Kent worked on Dickens' subsequent reading tours. "[H]e had in an extraordinary degree the dramatic element in his character. It was an integral part of his individuality. It colored his whole temperament or idiosyncracy."

"The secret of his original success, and of the long sustainment of it in each of these two careers—as Writer and as Reader—is in a great measure discoverable in this, that whatever powers he possessed he applied to their very uttermost. Whether as Author or as Impersonator, he gave himself up to his appointed task, not partially or intermittingly, but thoroughly and indefatigably," remembered Kent.

The Birmingham Journal reported on "how Mr. Dickens twirled his moustache, or played with his paper knife, or laid down his book, and leaned confidently. . . ."

"[H]e consented to read his *Carol* a second time, on Friday the 30th, if seats were reserved for working men at prices within their means," wrote Forster. Two thousand people attended.

Dickens thought the third audience was the best of the three. This reading had been especially priced for working men and women. "They lost nothing, followed everything closely, laughed and cried," Dickens himself reported, "and animated me to that extent that I felt as if we were all bodily going up into the clouds together."

According to the *Birmingham Journal*, Dickens mounted the stage, and before he began his reading, stepped forward and began by addressing them as "My good friends. . . ." But he had to stop, because immediately there was "a perfect hurricane of applause."

He continued, telling his audience that he had always wished "To have the great pleasure of meeting you face to face at this Christmas time. If ever there was a time when any one class could of itself do much for its own good, and for the welfare of society—which I greatly doubt—that time is unquestionably past. It is in the fusion of different classes, without confusion; in the bringing together of employers and employed; in the creating of a better common understanding among those whose interests are identical, who depend upon each other, and who can never be in unnatural antagonism without deplorable results, that one of our chief principles of a Mechanic's Institution should consist."

Dickens concluded his introduction, saying, "I now proceed to the pleasant task to which I assure you I have looked forward now for a long time."

"Marley was dead . . ." Dickens began again.

After the recitation was over, and the immense applause had died down, the performer again spoke directly to the audience, saying, ". . . I am truly and sincerely interested in you . . . any service to you I have freely rendered from my heart. . . ."

The result was an addition of between £400 and £500 to the funds for establishment of the new Institute.

A prettily worked silver flower-basket, presented to Mrs. Dickens, commemorated these first public readings "to nearly six thousand people, and the design they had generously helped," wrote Forster years later.

The result of the performances was so fantastic, and the word spread so quickly, that Dickens was deluged with requests to perform the same feats elsewhere. Dickens at first refused requests that offered payments or honorariums, protesting that it was not right for a novelist to perform.

"If Dickens does turn Reader he will make another fortune. He will never offer to do so, of course. But if they will have him he will do it, he told me today," wrote a friend of Dickens later.

Eventually, Dickens came around to these requests and became one of the first novelists of his generation to perform his own works in such a way. When he eventually changed his mind and began giving public readings as a means of support, he was able to make more money than he had ever known as a novelist, and became one of the first modern celebrities of the age.

The Last Christmas

"The *Carol* also shows a notable development in the consciously autobiographical element in Dickens' writing. The story actually turns on memory, specifically on the deleterious consequences of blanking out one's own past, as he himself had often fantasized about doing," wrote biographer Michael Slater. "As a writer, Dickens cannot yet, it seems, directly confront the blacking factory itself but nevertheless comes closer here to the factual truth of his boyhood sufferings than ever before."

Would this be the Christmas that he would finally confront those memories?

Dickens had been in poor health. He had battled foot infections the last five years of his life, sometimes due to his own bad habits of walking in the snow and rain and not taking off his boots, causing massive pain.

On September 2, 1867, he wrote to *The Times* denying rumors of illness, and the next day wrote to a friend, "I never was better in my life—doubt if anybody ever was or can be better—and have not had anything the matter with me but that squeezed foot, which was an affair of a few days."

On Christmas Day, 1869, Charles Dickens' foot was so swollen that he could not leave his room. It was too painful to walk, and he only hobbled down at the end of the day to join in the family's festivities after Christmas dinner.

He laid on the sofa in the drawing room, with his family filling the room with conversation and laughter. He watched them play parlor games. This was his favorite part of the season, but with his strength sapped it was a difficult time for him.

As Andre Maurois wrote many years later, "Dickens was lying ill on a sofa, playing with his children a simple game known to the family as the 'memory game.' It consisted of accumulating in turn words or phrases with no link of association. . . ."

It was one of Dickens' favorite games. On this specific night, Dickens' son Henry, who went on to become a very successful barrister, remembered a very important moment. He was twenty years old at the time. After several turns watching, Dickens could not help but join in the game even from his prone position.

"My father, after many turns had successfully gone through the long string of words and finished up with his own contribution, 'Warren's Blacking, 30 Strand.' He gave this with an odd twinkle in his eye and a strange inflection in his voice which at once forcibly arrested my attention and left a vivid impression on my mind for some time afterwards," recalled Henry.

It was the address of the blacking factory where Dickens had withstood the immense hurt of being sent to work while still a child. "The site of his childhood labor and humiliation. The source of all his agony. And yet the name meant nothing to his family; none of them knew of his past. Just another phrase in the course of a Christmas game, but, to Dickens, how pregnant with the whole mystery of his life," wrote Ackroyd.

A young Charles Dickens laboring at the blacking factory.

Referring to Warren's blacking, Michael and Mollie Hardwick wrote that "the damage had been done. Until old Hungerford Market was pulled down, and the old Hungerford Stairs and the rotting old house were destroyed, Dickens never had the courage to go near them, either as a youth or man."

"As Dickens grew up he became eager for success and security, and he quickly acquired the manners of a gentleman. Yet he remained compulsively fascinated by his suppressed experience. It had formed an indissoluble bond of sympathy, even of identity, with the homeless, the friendless, the orphans, the hungry, the uneducated, and even the prisoners of London's lower depths. His childhood had been lost there and all his wanderings were a search for it," wrote Norman and Jeanne MacKenzie.

"It was a very long time before I liked to go up Chandos Street. My old way home by the Borough made me cry, even after my eldest child could speak," Dickens wrote many years later.

Dickens did not explain his choice of words in the game, and no one pressed him. In fact, none of them would know about the boot black factory until they (and the public) read about it in Forster's biography several years later.

"It was not until his biography appeared, after his death, that they remembered those words which he had spoken with such curious reluctance, and yet unable to stop himself, and realized that they were the address of the blacking factory where he had toiled to keep his family when his father was in prison," wrote Maurois.

"All that his readers knew or surmised about Dickens' childhood, apart from the glimpse they had been given in the Cheap Edition preface to *Nicholas Nickleby* . . . they would have derived a generalized impression of a secure middle-class background. . . ." wrote biographer Michael Slater. "Forster's first volume therefore came as a revelation indeed. . . . Certainly the reviewers found much in Dickens's powerfully written account of what Forster calls his 'hard experiences in boyhood' that explained why he developed into the kind of novelist that he did."

"Thrown among the poor and needy, and sympathizing with all their sufferings, he handled their sorrows as one of themselves, and this was more than enough to counterbalance the fact that he lacked 'the manners of a gentleman,' " remarked the *Times* of Forster's version of Dickens' childhood.

"Certain biographers have shown surprise at his reticence concerning this period of his life, and regarded his painful sensibility as proof of a rather despicable vanity. These critics can never have experienced humiliation in their own childhood. It is a fine thing for a man to be wise when, in the course of a long life, he has painfully formed his own wisdom; but how foolish it is to expect spontaneous wisdom from a child! And when a child has suffered, as Dickens did, a change of caste, he must be superhuman if he is left unscathed," wrote Maurois.

Henry never forgot. Many years later, at family Christmas gatherings at Henry Dickens' home at 8 Mulberry Walk in London, he performed imitations of his father giving his famous "Readings," during which he would wear a geranium, his father's favorite flower, and lean on the same velvet-covered reading stand used by Charles Dickens during his reading tours. He had listened to his father many times, and older members of his audience said Henry Dickens' performances were amazingly like those given by his father. To celebrate his eightieth birthday in 1929, Henry went through the whole of A Christmas Carol without a hitch, his false teeth loosening at the melodramatic sections. In October 1914 he performed the recitals of his father's works in support of the Red Cross Society. These included excerpts from *David Copperfield*, *A Christmas Carol*, *The Chimes*, and *The Cricket on the Hearth*. Through his efforts he raised £1,200 for the Society.

But in the end, the hurt little boy, except for a few insightful releases such as the one made to Forster, stayed safely locked in Charles Dickens' heart. The little boy who walked about London, afraid, hungry, hurt, alone, and insecure, it turned out, had forever stayed in the little garret on Bayham Street.

The Last Reading

"No one can imagine their own death, even when they know it is coming," wrote literary historian Claire Tomalin of Dickens in 1870, when he was fifty-eight years old. "Dickens rejected and defied his illness with a spirit that would not flinch or budge. At the same time he sensed danger and set about putting order into his affairs—family matters, money, copyrights. His days were now packed with business meetings, readings, public and private . . . there were speeches to deliver, dinners and receptions . . . social obligations to insistent friends, to politicians and even to royalty. . . ."

As he had done throughout the rest of his speaking career, the book he performed most often was *A Christmas Carol.*

Without question, he had become a professional speaker. He usually included all the Christmas books in his vast repertoire, as well as selections from *Dombey and Son*, *Nicholas Nickleby*, *The Pickwick Papers*, *Martin Chuzzlewit*, and *David Copperfield*.

Dickens biographer Edgar Johnson wrote, "It was more than a reading; it was an extraordinary exhibition of acting . . . without a single prop or bit of costume, by changes of voice, by gesture, by vocal expression, Dickens peopled his stage with a throng of characters."

"What creatures were those who, one by one—sometimes, it almost seemed, two or three of them together—appeared and disappeared upon the platform, at the Reader's own good-will and pleasure!" remembered Charles Kent. On the other hand, as Kent explained, Dickens abbreviated the text for his readings. "The descriptive passages were cut out by wholesale. While the Christmas dinner at Scrooge's Clerk's, and the Christmas party at Scrooge's Nephew's, were left in almost in their entirety, the street-scenes and shop-window displays were obliterated altogether."

"He tightened the narrative, wrote stage directions to himself in the margins, and tried to infuse as much humor as possible, leaving out passages of social criticism as inappropriate for evenings of entertainment," wrote Dickens historian David Perdue. "Thomas Carlyle, author and friend of Dickens, after attending one of the readings, remarked that Dickens was like an entire theater company . . . under one hat.

"Dickens' six-man entourage for these reading tours included his manager (Albert Smith, later George Dolby), a valet, a gas man, and a couple of others doing clerical work and odd jobs. The unique stage equipment included a reading desk, carpet, gas lights, and screens behind to help project his voice forward."

After many discussions and many concerns, Dickens had agreed to take on a reading tour of America, from December 1867 to April 1868, which earned him £19,000—a huge sum. But the grueling pace of the schedule and the demands of the performances (and the attenuated social gatherings before and after) sapped his already dwindling strength and worsened his health considerably.

It was a young Mark Twain, who sat in the audience in January 1858, still a correspondent for the *San Francisco Alta California*, who filed a dispatch for that newspaper.

"I only heard him read once," Twain wrote. "It was in New York, last week. I had a seat about the middle of Steinway Hall, and that was rather further away from the speaker than was pleasant or profitable.

"Promptly at 8 p.m., unannounced, and without waiting for any stamping or clapping of hands to call him out, a tall, 'spry,' (if I may say it,) thin-legged old gentleman, gotten up regardless of expense, especially as to shirt-front and diamonds, with a bright red flower in his button-hole, gray beard and moustache, bald head, and with side hair brushed fiercely and tempestuously forward, as if its owner were sweeping down before a gale of wind, the very Dickens came! He did not emerge upon the stage—that is rather too deliberate a word—he strode. He strode—in the most English way and exhibiting the most English general style and appearance—straight across the broad stage, heedless of everything, unconscious of everybody, turning neither to the right nor the left—but striding eagerly straight ahead, as if he had seen a girl he knew turn the next corner.

"Mr. Dickens had a table to put his book on, and on it he had also a tumbler, a fancy decanter and a small bouquet. Behind him he had a huge red screen—a bulkhead—a sounding-board, I took it to be—and overhead in front was suspended a long board with reflecting lights attached to it, which threw down a glory upon the gentleman, after the fashion in use in the picture-galleries for bringing out the best effects of great paintings. Style!— There is style about Dickens, and style about all his surroundings.

"Henry Wadsworth Longfellow attended the Boston readings with his family that same year. He and Dickens remained friends from his first visit, and remained so. Longfellow's daughter, Annie Allegra, attended the readings with her father and later recalled 'How the audience loved best of all the *Christmas Carol*' and how they laughed as Dickens fairly smacked his lips as there came the 'smell like an eating house and a pastry cook's next door to each other, with a laundress's next door to that,' as Mrs. Cratchit bore in the Christmas pudding and how they nearly wept as Tiny Tim cried 'God bless us every one!' " wrote Twain.

After his tour of America, Dickens pressed himself and, despite declining health, began a farewell tour of Britain in October 1868. Again, the tour was very lucrative and at the same time increased his popularity.

Dickens in performance.

In fact, his readings had caused a major sensation when he decided to work in a reading of the death of Nancy at the hands of Bill Sikes, from *Oliver Twist*. Sensational stories of women fainting filled the box-office receipts. At some readings, police were required to control the attending mobs.

According to Perdue, "This tour included a new addition, a very passionate and dramatic performance of the murder of Nancy from *Oliver Twist*. Many believe that [Dickens was affected by] the energy expended in this performance, which he insisted on including even as his health worsened. . . ."

The following year, on April 20, 1869, Dickens had to cut a provincial tour short after collapsing and showing symptoms of a mild stroke. When he had regained sufficient strength, he arranged, with medical approval, for a series of readings to partially make up to Chappell & Co. (the tour sponsors) what they had lost due to his illness. Twelve final performances were scheduled, running from January 11, 1870, to his last public reading at 8 p.m. on March 15, 1870.

This final reading was at St. James Hall in London that opened on March 25, 1858. It was designed by architect and artist Owen Jones who had also decorated the interior of the Crystal Palace. It was situated between the quadrant of Regent Street and Piccadilly, and Vine Street and George Court. There was a frontage on Regent Street, and another in Piccadilly. Taking the orchestra into account, the main hall had seating for slightly over 2,000 people. The immense hall was decorated in the Florentine style, with features imitating the great Moorish Palace of the Alhambra. The Piccadilly facade was given a Gothic design. Sir George Henschel recalled its "dear old, uncomfortable, long, narrow, green-upholstered benches (made of pale-green horse-hair) with the numbers of the seats tied over the straight backs with bright pink tape, like office files." From a year after its opening, and for almost half a century thereafter, the St. James Hall was London's principal concert hall.

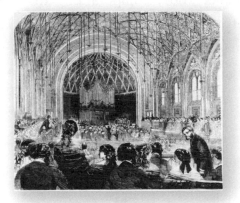

St. James Hall.

Dickens had given, by some estimates, 444 readings around the world and had earned the then astonishing sum of £93,000. And it was no accident that the last readings he had given during the American tour were those of *A Christmas Carol* as well. "Dickens' public readings were by far the most successful one-man show of the nineteenth century. . . . In the twelve years of the Readings Dickens had barnstormed across Britain and America being greeted by idolatrous audiences wherever he appeared, but the Final Farewell Reading was the crowning triumph," wrote Victorian chronicler Raymund Fitzsimons.

"It was an occasion of high emotion for reader and public," wrote Tomalin. "Crowds were turned away at the door as an audience of 2,000 gathered inside, many paying only a shilling for a seat, and when he came on to the platform they rose to their feet to cheer him."

In December 1869, compounding his foot problem, Dickens' left hand was sporadically painful. And by mid- to late-January 1870 he had started wearing a sling, and all throughout February his hand was in constant pain.

Charles Dickens late in life.

Friends, such as London columnist Edmund Yates, could not understand how a man who had lent such time and support to science and education could mislead himself so badly about his condition. "Never did [a] man wishing to deceive himself carry out his object so thoroughly as Dickens. . . . What would he have thought, what would he have said, of any other man who could only read half the letters of the names over the shop-doors, who 'found himself extremely giddy and extremely uncertain of the sense of touch, both in the left leg and the left hand and arm,' and who ascribed those symptoms 'to the effect of medicine'? With what caustic touches would he have described a man who, suffering under all those symptoms, and under many others equally significant, harassed, worn out, yet travels and reads and works until he falls dead on the roadside!"

Dickens' doctor, Frank Beard, attributed many of Dickens' maladies, especially his foot, to gout. Yet Dickens pressed on. Beard was so worried for Dickens' health that he insisted Dickens' son Charles be in the front row just in case his father collapsed or seized up, telling Charles, "I have had some steps put up the side of the platform. You must be there every night, and if you see your father falter in the least, you must run up and catch him and bring him off with me, or, by Heaven, he'll die before them all."

On many nights during that final run of readings,

Dickens had to be helped back to his dressing room during the intermission, as his heart raced and his body failed. He would rest, prostrate, throughout the full allotted time.

Despite all this constant and rightful worry, Dickens went about his business. But even he knew it was the end of an era.

"The time had now come for him to prepare himself for his final reading, his last appearance before the public. Two days before, he gave a dinner for all those connected with the business side of the reading tours, and then, on March 15, he prepared for his final reading. He was suffering from a bad throat," wrote Peter Ackroyd.

At 8 p.m. Dickens ascended the stage.

"The largest audience ever assembled in that immense building, the largest, as already intimated, that ever can be assembled there for purely Reading purposes, namely, when the orchestra and the upper end of the two side-galleries have necessarily to be barred or curtained off from the auditorium, were collected together there under the radiant pendants of the glittering ceiling, every available nook and corner, and all the ordinary gangways of the Great Hall being completely occupied," remembered Charles Kent.

There were friends and family in the front row. Included in the throng was his little six-year-old granddaughter Mary Angela Dickens, whom he adoringly called "Mekitty," there to hear her grandfather perform for the first time. She was frightened by the man who stood on stage, whom she called "Venerables" (all his grandchildren called him that), as he spoke in "unknown voices" and made scary faces.

There were huge crowds outside the two entrances to the theater on Regent Street and Piccadilly. He began the reading punctually at 8 p.m. by walking onto the stage with the book in hand. He seemed much agitated, as much by his other maladies as by his throat.

The crowd roared to life, cheering and rising to their feet. So great was the noise that Dickens stood there, behind his desk, smiling, unable to start until the loud ovation had subsided.

George Dolby, the stage manager, remembered Dickens' "spare figure . . . faultlessly attired in evening dress, the gas-light streaming down upon him, illuminating every feature of his familiar flushed face. . . ."

After a brief greeting, he began, "Marley was dead. . . ."

"The different original characters introduced in his stories, when he read them, he did not simply describe, he impersonated: otherwise to put it, for whomsoever he spoke, he spoke in character," remembered Charles Kent.

Dickens biographer Claire Tomalin described Dolby as "a big man, full of energy, optimism and know-how, and talkative, with a stammer he bravely disregarded. He was thirty-five, just married, a theatre manager out of work and keen to take on the running of Dickens' . . . reading tour. He was sent by Chappell, the music publishers who were setting up the tour, and he won Dickens' confidence at once, and quickly became a friend. . . . They laughed and joked together like boys, and enjoyed the small rituals of travel."

Dolby wrote about Dickens' performances, "The scenes in which appeared Tiny Tim (a special favorite with him) affected him and his audience alike, and it not infrequently happened that he was interrupted by loud sobs from the female portion of his audience (and occasionally, too, from men) who, perhaps, had experienced the inexpressible grief of losing a child. So artistically was this reading arranged, and so rapid was the transition from grave to gay, that his hearers had scarcely time to dry their eyes after weeping before they were enjoying the fun of Scrooge's discovery of Christmas Day, and his conversation from his window with the boy in the court below. All these points told with wonderful effect, the irresistible manner of the reader enhancing a thousand times the subtle magic with which the *Carol* is written."

"[T]he old delicacy was now again delightfully manifest, and a subdued tone, as well in the humorous as the serious portions, gave something to all the reading as of a quiet sadness of farewell. The charm of this was at its height when he shut the volume . . . and spoke in his own person," Forster recalled. "He said that for fifteen years he had been reading his own books to audiences whose sensitive and kindly recognition of them had given him instruction and enjoyment in his art such as few men could have had; but that he nevertheless thought it well now to retire upon older associations, and in future to devote himself exclusively to the calling which had first made him known."

There were a few mistakes: Dickens could not seem to pronounce Pickwick, saying instead Pickswick, Pecknicks, or Pickwicks. He finished the reading to great fanfare, and as he turned to exit the stage, the crowd called him back again, and again, begging for a final word.

"Ladies and Gentlemen, it would be worse than idle—for it would be hypocritical and unfeeling—if I were to disguise that I close this episode in my life with feelings of very considerable pain," Dickens began. "For some fifteen years in this hall, and in many kindred places, I have had the honor of presenting my own cherished ideas before you for your recognition, and in closely observing your reception of them have enjoyed an amount of artistic delight and instruction, which perhaps it is given to few men to know. In this task and in every other I have ever undertaken as a faithful servant of the public, always imbued with the sense of duty to them, and always striving to do his best, I have been uniformly cheered by the readiest response, the most generous sympathy, and the most stimulating support. Nevertheless, I have thought it well, at the full flood-tide of your favor, to retire upon those older associations between us, which date from much further back than these, thenceforth to devote myself exclusively to the art that first brought us together."

He hesitated.

"In but two short weeks from this time I hope that you may enter, in your own homes, on a new series of readings at which my assistance will be indispensable," Dickens spoke haltingly yet with raw emotion, "but from these garish lights I vanish now for evermore, with a heartfelt, grateful, respectful, affectionate farewell."

"The manly, cordial voice only faltered once at the very last," wrote Charles Kent. "The mournful modulation of it in the utterance of the words, 'From these garish lights I vanish now for evermore,' lingers to this moment like a haunting melody in our remembrance."

"When he ceased to speak," wrote Henry Fielding Dickens, sixty years later, "a kind of sigh seemed to come from the audience, followed almost at once by such a storm of cheering as I have never seen equaled in my life. He was deeply touched that night, but infinitely sad and broken."

Tears streamed down Dickens' face as the applause continued without let up. Mekitty recalled years later how upset she was: "I count among the most distressful moments of my childish existence, the moment when

'Venerables' cried. There is an element of distress in my last picture, but there is a smile in it too. And I am always glad I have it—that I have that one impression of my grandfather in connection with the public that loved him, and loves him still."

He tried something like a smile. He left, but the crowd insisted on another bow. He came back out and blew a giant kiss to the audience and left again for the final time.

"The brief hush of silence as he moved from the platform; and the prolonged tumult of sound that followed suddenly, stayed him, and again for another moment brought him back; will not be forgotten by any present," concluded Forster.

Charles Dickens died on June 9, 1870. His funeral card read: "From these garish lights I vanish now for evermore."

A Christmas Wish

The following sentiment was offered by Charles Dickens to his children. Mamie closed the Christmas chapter of her book with it, and it only seems appropriate to do so here now:

"Reflect upon your present blessings—of which every man has many—not on your past misfortunes, of which all men have some. Fill your glass again with a merry face and contented heart. Our life on it, but your Christmas shall be merry and your New Year a happy one.

"So may the New Year be a happy one to you, happy to many more whose happiness depends on you! So may each year be happier than the last, and not the meanest of our brethren or sisterhood debarred their rightful share in what our great Creator formed them to enjoy."

Acknowledgements

Any author of such an effort owes a great debt of gratitude to those who went before him. Several writers' works have proved invaluable, including those of John Forster, Michael Slater, Peter Ackroyd, Stephen Leacock, Andre Maurois, Claire Tomalin, Edgar Johnson, and many more, and of course Dickens' children Mamie Dickens and Charles Dickens Jr. as well as his granddaughter Mekitty.

I poured over more than five hundred original sources, including diaries, letters, and interviews with Dickens, his children, their household members, and biographies of friends and literary partners, searching for hints of Christmas here and there to weave into this story.

As ever, I owe a debt of special thanks in all of my professional endeavors to Gilbert King for his ear, opinions, advice, general good cheer, and encouragement. Others who also cheered me on were Michael Fragnito and Caitlin Friedman, among others.

I would, of course, like to thank John Whalen of Cider Mill Press Book Publishers, who helped make this book a reality. Were it not for his excitement, enthusiasm, and faith in me, I might have given up under the weight of this massive project. I also owe a huge debt of gratitude to Alyssa Richard, Alex Smith, and Greg Jones who helped mold a rather large manuscript into readable shape, and to Alicia Freile who managed the design. Thanks also to Whitney Cookman for a wonderful dust-jacket design.

I would like to thank my family, especially my sons, Dylan and Dawson, whom I have taken too much time away from in order to pursue not only this work, but also my other professional aspirations. I have tried to attend as many of their basketball, baseball, and track competitions as possible, but there is no replacement for a catch in the yard or an ice-cream cone, many of which were robbed by my other pursuits. I vow to them to spend more time hanging out and less time working.

End Notes

PROLOGUE

Brown, Joel, 'Christmas Carol' passes from one Dickens to another, *The Boston Globe* (Boston, MA) December 19, 2013

Temple Theater, http://www.tremonttemple.org/ourstory

Wikipedia, http://en.wikipedia.org/wiki/Tremont_Temple

THE TRAIN RIDE

"There is a hackney-coach . . . Dickens, Charles, *Charles Dickens on London*, Miniature Masterpieces, 2013

"*Chuzzlewit* had fallen short. . . Forster, John, *The Life of Charles Dickens*, Sterling Publishing (New York, NY) 2011

"It is not uncommon though. . . Smiley, Jane, *Charles Dickens*, Viking (New York, NY) 2002

Dickens probably scheduled. . . Railway Schedules of the London & Birmingham, 1843

"I think I must be the. . . Noden, Merrell, "Frisky as the Dickens," *Sports Illustrated*, February 15, 1988

"Houses were knocked. . . Johnson, Edgar, *Charles Dickens, His Tragedy and Triumph, Vol I & II*, Simon & Schuster (New York, NY) 1952

"when I wanted variety. . . Nordquist, Richard, "Night Walks," by Charles Dickens, http://grammar.about.com/od/classicessays/a/nightwalks_4.htm

"The Dickens lived in what. . . Callow, Simon, *Dickens' Christmas: A Victorian Celebration*, Frances Lincoln (London, England) 2009

"His schoolboy's few clothes . . . Kaplan, Fred, *Dickens: A Biography*, William Morrow & Co. (New York, NY) 1990

And this I know, Dickens, Charles, Speech in support of the Manchester Athenaeum, October 5, 1843

"This was a dream, also . . . Ackroyd, Peter, *Dickens*, Harper Collins (New York, NY) 1990

"I could not bear to think . . . Tomalin, Claire, *Charles Dickens: A Life*, The Penguin Press (New York, NY) 2011

"not caring to be under. . . Johnson

"We were indebted for. . . Ackroyd

"I shall enforce the. . . Standiford, Les, *The Man Who Invented Christmas*, Broadway Books (New York, NY) 2008

"How often have we. . . Dickens speech, 1843

"The soiree of the next. . . Ackroyd

"Something about 'the bright. . . Johnson, Edgar, *Charles Dickens: His Tragedy and Triumph*, abridgement, Puffin (New York, NY) 1986

"Active as he had been. . . Forster

STAVE I

EBENEZER SCROOGE

"None of Dickens characters. . . Sanders, Andrew, *Charles Dickens's London*, Robert Hale (London, England) 2010

"For Dickens, London was. . . Sanders

"I have been this. . . Forster

"This was his first. . . Forster

But the gloaming of an evening. . . "Revealed: the Scot who inspired Dickens' Scrooge," *The Scotsman* (Edinburgh, Scotland) April 24, 2014

Ebenezer Scrooge. . . http://historum.com/blogs/chookie/580-ebeneezer-scrooge.html

John Meggott Elwes. . . Topham, Edward, The Life of the Late John Elwes, Esquire, Paraclete Potter (Poughkeepsie, NY) 1790

"complained bitterly of the birds. . . Miller, William Haig, The Culture of Pleasure, Robert Carter & Bros. (New York, NY) 1873

In 1772 with the help. . . http://en.wikipedia.org/wiki/John_Elwes_(politician)

"He was halfway through. . . Smiley

SCROOGE AND MARLEY

"It was within this maze. . . Jones, Richard, Walking Dickensian London, Interlink Books (London, England) 2005

"the ancient tower of a. . . Rattigan, David L., "Where was Scrooge's Office?," http://scroogebook.blogspot.com/2011/10/where-was-scrooges-office.html

Newman's Court is off the. . . Hoole, Ivor, "A guide to the alleys, courts, passages, and yards of central London" http://www.ianvisits.co.uk/london-alleys/

Newman's Court first became. . . McCullough, John Ramsay, A Dictionary, Practical, Theoretical, and Historical of Commerce, Longman, Brown, Green & Longmans (London, England) 1852

FRED

"Furnival's Inn was inhabited. . . Johnson Vol. 1

"into an uncarpeted and. . . Johnson Vol. 1

"The Doughty Street home. . . Johnson Vol. 1

"mahogany doors, bookshelves. . . Tomalin

THE SOLICITORS

"The power of population. . . Malthus T. R., *An Essay on the Principle of Population*, Chapter VII, 1798

"I don't believe now. . . Forster

"The great Malthusian dread. . . Ritschel, Dr. Dan, Center for History Education at the University of Maryland, http://www. umbc.edu/history/CHE/InstPg/RitDop/Discovery-of-poverty-Malthusianism.htm

BOB CRATCHIT

"I thought in the little back. . . Tyler, Daniel, *A Guide to Dickens London*, Hesperus Press (London, England) 2012

"Bayham Street was about the. . . Forster

"The housing was uninspiring. . . Tyler

"To say. . . Johnson, Vol 1.

"To be sure the Cratchits. . . Nissenbaum, Stephen, *The Battle for Christmas*, Vintage Books (New York, NY) 1996

"Most people walked. . . Sanders

"These tended to be. . . Sanders

"Cities fostered new breeds. . . Amato, Anthony, *On Foot: A History of Walking*, New York University Press (New York, NY) 2004

"[The] core was the old. . . Poole, Daniel, *What Jane Austen Ate and What Charles Dickens Knew*, Simon & Schuster (New York, NY) 1993

"In Jane Austen's day. . . Poole

JACOB MARLEY

"a private gentleman and. . . Ackroyd

"Dickens's walks served him. . . Noden

"But Dickens's walks played. . . Noden

"If I could not walk far. . . Noden

"Legend holds that it was. . . Jones

"It should not be imagined. . . Johnson, Vol. 1

There was a marked difference. . . MacKenzie, Norman and Jeanne, *Dickens: A Life*, Oxford University Press (New York, NY) 1979

"dragged by the hair of my head. . . Ackroyd

"All through the Christian ages. . . Orwell, George, Charles Dickens, Inside the Whale and Other Essays, Penguin (London, England) 1940

STAVE II

THE GHOST OF CHRISTMAS PAST

"His study had to be precisely. . . Currey, Mason, *Daily Rituals*, Alfred A. Knopf (New York, NY) 2014

"On an ordinary day, he. . . Currey

"I have never forgotten. . . Hearn, Michael Patrick, *The Annotated Christmas Carol*, W.W. Norton (New York, NY) 2004

"The scheme of A. . . Hearn

"As with every other. . . Hearn

THE SCHOOL

"every encouragement in his power. . . Langton, Robert, *The Childhood and Youth of Charles Dickens*, Cornell University Library (Ithaca, NY) 2012

Students at Mr. Giles' school were. . . Langton

"The school room setting. . . Slater

"Those who seek reasons. . . Ackroyd

"in the days when there. . . Langton

OLD FEZZIWIG

"When we were only babies. . . Dickens, Mamie, *My Father, As I Recall Him*, Roxburghe Press (Westminster, England) 1896

"No one can imagine. . . Dickens, Mamie

"The relationship between the. . . Nissenbaum

BELLE

"Hogarth. . . had a large and still. . . Tomalin

"He (Dickens) saw in her. . . Tomalin

"I am writing by candle-light. . . Ackroyd

"All the whilehe was trying. . . MacKenzie

"You know . . . I have. . . Ackroyd

"Kate," wrote Edgar Johnson, "finding that . . . Johnson

"the quantity is not sufficient. . . Johnson

"with what a strange mastery. . . Forster

STAVE III

CHRISTMAS PRESENT

"I am bent on paying the money. . . Forster

"Leech was a nervous. . . Hearn

"As a child Charles was exposed. . . Perdue, David, "Dickens' Amateur Theatricals," http://charlesdickenspage.com/stage.html

"Constantly underfed, Charles sniffed. . . Kaplan, Michael, *Charles Dickens*, Yale University Press (New Haven, CT) 2009

". . . I fell into a state of neglect. . . Ackroyd

"Workers with some income. . . Poole

". . . others observed that Dickens'. . . Douglas-Fairhurst, Robert, *Becoming Dickens*, Belknap Harvard University Press (Boston, MA) 2009

"That image of everyone sitting. . . Kirka, Danica, "Dickens Christmas: A turkey as big as me? What's at Tiny Tim's table?" *Lubbock Avalanche-Journal*, December 21, 2008

"Narrative snapshots like the. . . Douglas-Fairhurst

TINY TIM

"Harry was a singular child. . . Ackroyd

"The blackened skies would. . . Chesney, Russell W., M.D., "Environmental factors in Tiny Tim's near-fatal illness," *Archives of Pediatrics and Adolescent Medicine*, March 2012

"The salary earned by Bob Cratchit. . . Chesney

"The dependent person with a disability. . . Block, Laurie with Alison, Jay, producers, "Inventng the Poster Child," NPR. org, http://www.npr.org/programs/disability/ba_shows.dir/ pos_chld.dir/highlights/ttim.html

THE MINERS

"From October 27, to 4 November 1842. . . Slater

"his imagination continued to be. . . Slater

"Christmas was always a. . . Kaplan

"The close, low chamber at the back. . . Dickens, Charles, "Field Lane Ragged School," *Daily News* (London) February 4, 1846

". . . [H]e saw before him always. . . Ackroyd

"Many of them retire for. . . Kaplan

STAVE IV

"In the play Everyman, death. . . Bolton, Daniel, "The Study
   of Death in 'The Summoning of Everyman,' " http://voices.
   yahoo.com/the-study-death-summoning-everyman-10726313.
   html, December 22, 2011

THE EXCHANGE

"The Royal Exchange was opened. . . Dickens, Charles, Jr.,
   Dickens's Dictionary of London, 1879

THE PAWNBROKER

". . . nobody ever came to the school. . . Ackroyd

". . . [H]is distracted mother tried. . . Johnson, Vol. 1

"Charles, as the man of the family. . . Tomalin

THE DEATH OF TINY TIM

"It was feared, but regarded with . . . Manoli-Skocay, Constance,
   "A Gentle Death: Tuberculosis in 19th Century Concord,"
   The Concord Magazine, Winter, 2003

STAVE V

"Marley's Ghost is the symbol. . . Johnson

"In A *Christmas Carol* Dickens imagines. . . Ackroyd

"In fact, as everyone surely knew. . . Baker, Russell, "Did Scrooge
   Buy a Goose or Turkey?" *The Register-Guard* (Eugene,
   Oregon) January 20, 1986

"So, the turkey that Scrooge purchased. . . Rubel, William,
   http://www.williamrubel.com/2006/07/07/charles-dickens-
   and-turkeys/, July 7, 2006

THE SOLICITOR REDUX

"The truth is that Dickens's criticism. . . Orwell

BOB CRATCHIT'S RAISE

"I assume if somebody else. . . Gollom, Mark, "Scrooge an economic hero, defenders say," CBC News, http://www. cbc.ca/news/canada/scrooge-an-economic-hero-defenders-say-1.1161205, December 21, 2012

"many thousands whose jobs . . . Gollom

TINY TIM

"How could Scrooge, who. . . Chesney

EPILOGUE

"This was a primitive process. . . Hearn

"I do not doubt, in my own. . . Hearn

"At Christmas 1843 Dickens, for all. . . Tomalin

"Dickens and Forster above all exerted . . . Carlyle, Jane, http://carlyleletters.dukejournals.org/

"Forster is out again; and if he don't. . . Ackroyd

"Good God, how we missed you. . . Johnson

"Never had a little book an outset. . . Forster

"The book went straight to. . . Tomalin

"A few days later, in a separate. . . Wagenknecht, Edward, *Dickens and the Scandalmongers*, University of Oklahoma Press (Norman, OK) 1965

"He was one of the oddest men to. . . Callow

"Christmas cards were not introduced . . . Ackroyd

"Dickens, with his *A Christmas Carol*, more than. . . Connelly, Mark, *Christmas, A History*, I.B. Tauris & Co. (London, England) 2012

DISAPPOINTMENT. . .

Dickens soon found himself in a . . . Ackroyd

"The first six thousand copies . . . Forster

"And indeed this was his panic . . . Ackroyd

THE FIRST READING

"the coxcombical idea of writing down . . . Johnson

"On the way to the railway station. . . Ackroyd

". . . we were all going on together. . . Ackroyd

"Dickens's delighted enjoyment, in fact. . . Kent, Charles, *Charles Dickens as a Reader*, Chapman & Hall, 1872

"The secret of his original success. . . Kent

"how Mr. Dickens twirled his moustache. . . Ackroyd,

"My good friends. . . ." But he had to stop. . . Ackroyd

"I now proceed to the pleasant task. . . Ackroyd

"If Dickens does turn Reader. . . Ackroyd

THE LAST CHRISTMAS

"The Carol also shows a notable. . . Slater

"Dickens was lying ill on a sofa, playing. . . Maurois, Andre, *Dickens*, Frederick Ungar Publishing (New York, NY) 1967

"My father, after man turns had successfully. . . Ackroyd

"As Dickens grew up. . . MacKenzie

"The site of his childhood labor. . . Ackroyd

"It was not until his biography appeared. . . Maurois

"All that his readers knew or. . . Slater

"Thrown among the poor and needy. . . Slater

"Certain biographers have shown surprise. . . Maurois

THE LAST READING

"No one can imagine their own. . . Tomalin

"It was more than a reading; it was an extraordinary. . . Johnson

"what creatures were those. . . Kent

"He tightened the narrative. . . Perdue, David, "Dickens' Public Readings," http://charlesdickenspage.com/stage.html

"Dickens' six-man entourage . . . Perdue, Public Readings

"How the audience loved best of all. . . Perdue, Public Readings

"It was an occasion of high emotion. . . Tomalin

"Never did [a] man wishing to deceive. . . McManus, I.C., "Charles Dickens: A Neglected Diagonosis," *The Lancet*, *Volume 358, Issue 9299*, pp. 2158 - 2161, December 22, 2001

"I have had some step put up the side. . . Johnson

"The time had now come for him. . . Ackroyd, p. 1066

"The largest audience ever assembled. . . Kent, Reader

"spare figure. . . faultlessly attired in evening dress. . . Ackroyd

"a big man, full of energy, optimism and know-how. . . Tomalin

"The manly, cordial voice only faltered. . . Kent, Readings

"When he ceased to speak," wrote Henry Fielding Dickens. . . Leacock, Stephen, *Charles Dickens: The Life and Work*, Doubleday Doran (Garden City, NY) 1936

"I count among the most distressful moments. . . Dickens, Mary Angela, "My Grandfather As I Knew Him," *Cosmopolitan*, *Volume 52*

Selected Bibliography

Ackroyd, Peter, *Dickens*, Harper Collins (New York, NY) 1990

Amato, Anthony, *On Foot: A History of Walking*, New York University Press (New York, NY) 2004

Baker, Russell, "Did Scrooge Buy a Goose or Turkey?" *The Register-Guard* (Eugene, Oregon) January 20, 1986

Bentley, Nicholas; Burgis, Nina; Slater, Michael, *The Dickens Index*, Ox ford University Press (New York, NY) 1990

Block, Laurie, with Alison, Jay, producers, "Inventng the Poster Child," NPR, http://www.npr.org/programs/disability/ba_ shows.dir/pos_chld.dir/highlights/ttim.html

Bolton, Daniel, "The Study of Death in 'The Summoning of Everyman'," http://voices.yahoo.com/the-study-death-summoning-everyman-10726313.html, December 22, 2011

Brown, Joel, " 'Christmas Carol' passes from one Dickens to another," *The Boston Globe* (Boston, MA) December 19, 2013

Callow, Simon, *Dickens' Christmas: A Victorian Celebration*, Frances Lincoln (London, England) 2009

Chesney, Russell W., M.D., "Environmental factors in Tiny Tim's near-fatal illness," *Archives of Pediatrics and Adolescent Medicine*, March 2012

Connelly, Mark, *Christmas, A History*, I.B. Tauris & Co. (London, England) 2012

Currey, Mason, *Daily Lives*, Alfred A. Knopf (New York, NY) 2014

Dickens, Charles, "Field Lane Ragged School," *Daily News* (London) February 4, 1846

Dickens, Charles, "Speech in support of the Manchester Athenaeum," October 5, 1843

Dickens, Charles, *My Early Times*, Compiled and Edited by Rowland, Peter, The Folio Society (London, England) 1988

Dickens, Charles, *Charles Dickens' on London*, Miniature Masterpieces, 2013

Dickens, Charles, Jr., *Dickens's Dictionary of London*, 1879

Dickens, Mamie, *My Father, As I Recall Him*, Roxburghe Press (Westminster, England) 1896

Dickens, Mary Angela, "My Grandfather As I Knew Him," *Cosmopolitan, Volume 52*

Douglas-Fairhurst, Robert, *Becoming Dickens*, Belknap Harvard University Press (Boston, MA) 2009

Fitzsimmons, Raymund, *The Charles Dickens Show*, Geoffrey Bles, London, England, 1970

Forster, John, edited by Holly Furneaux, *The Life of Charles Dickens*, Sterling Publishing (New York, NY) 2011

Golden, Morris, *Dickens Imagining Himself*, University Press of America (Lanham, MD) 1992

Gollom, Mark, "Scrooge an economic hero, defenders say," http://www.cbc.ca/news/canada/scrooge-an-economic-hero-defenders-say-1.1161205, December 21, 2012

Hardwick, Michael and Mollie, *Dickens's England*, J.M. Dent & Sons (London, England) 1970

Hearn, Michael Patrick, *The Annotated Christmas Carol*, W.W. Norton (New York, NY) 2004

Hoole, Ivor, "A guide to the alleys, courts, passages, and yards of central London" http://www.ianvisits.co.uk/london-alleys/

Johnson, Edgar, *Charles Dickens, His Tragedy and Triumph, Vol I & II*, Simon & Schuster (New York, NY) 1952

Johnson, Edgar, *Charles Dickens: His Tragedy and Triumph* (Abridgement), Puffin (New York, NY) 1986

Jones, Richard, *Walking Dickensian London*, Interlink Books (London, England) 2005

Kaplan, Fred, *Dickens: A Biography*, William Morrow & Co. (New York, NY) 1990

Kaplan, Michael, *Charles Dickens*, Yale University Press (New Haven, CT) 2009

Kent, Charles, *Charles Dickens as a Reader*, Chapman & Hall, 1872

Kirka, Danica, "Dickens Christmas: A turkey as big as me? What's at Tiny Tim's table?" *Lubbock Avalanche-Journal*, December 21, 2008

Langton, Robert, *The Childhood and Youth of Charles Dickens*, Cornell University Library (Ithaca, NY) 2012

Leacock, Stephen, *Charles Dickens: The Life and Work*, Doubleday Doran (Garden City, NY) 1936

McCullough, John Ramsay, *A Dictionary, Practical, Theoretical, and Historical of Commerce*, Longman, Brown, Green & Longmans (London, England) 1852

MacKenzie, Norman and Jeanne, *Dickens: A Life*, Oxford University Press (New York, NY) 1979

McManus, I.C., "Charles Dickens: A Neglected Diagnosis," *The Lancet*, Volume 358, Issue 9299, December 2001

Malthus T.R. 1798. *An Essay on the Principle of Population, Chapter VII*

Manoli-Skocay, Constance, "A Gentile Death: Tuberculosis in 19th Century Concord," *The Concord Magazine*, Winter, 2003

Maurois, Andre, *Dickens*, Frederick Ungar Publishing (New York, NY) 1967

Miller, William Haig, *The Culture of Pleasure, Or, the enjoyment of life in its Social Aspects*, Robert Carter & Bros. (New York, NY) 1873

Nissenbaum, Stephen, *The Battle for Christmas*, Vintage Books (New York, NY) 1996

Noden, Merrell, "Frisky as the Dickens," *Sports Illustrated*, February 15, 1998

Nordquist, Richard, "Night Walks," by Charles Dickens, http://grammar.about.com/od/classicessays/a/nightwalks_4.htm

Orwell, George, *Charles Dickens, Inside the Whale and Other Essays*, Penguin (London, England) 1940

Perdue, David, "Dickens' Amateur Theatricals,"http://charlesdickenspage.com/stage.html

Perdue, David, "Dickens' Public Readings," http://charlesdickenspage.com/stage.html

Poole, Daniel, *Dickens' Fur Coat and Charlotte's Unanswered Letters*, Harper Perennial (New York, NY) 1997

Poole, Daniel, *What Jane Austen Ate and What Charles Dickens Knew*, Simon & Schuster (New York, NY) 1993

Rattigan, David L., "Where was Scrooge's Office?" http://scroogebook.blogspot.com/2011/10/where-was-scrooges-office.html, October 13, 2011

Richardson, Ruth, *Dickens and the Workhouse: Oliver Twist and the London Poor*, Oxford University Press (New York, NY) 2012

Ritschel, Dr. Dan, Center for History Education at the University of Maryland, http://www.umbc.edu/history/CHE/InstPg/RitDop/Discovery-of-poverty-Malthusianism.htm

Rubel, William, "Charles Dickens and Turkeys," The Magic of Fire, Tradition and Foodways with William Rubel, http://www.williamrubel.com/2006/07/07/charles-dickens-and-turkeys/, July 7, 2006

Sanders, Andrew, *Charles Dickens's London*, Robert Hale (London, England) 2010

Smiley, Jane, *Charles Dickens*, Viking (New York, NY) 2002

Standiford, Les, *The Man Who Invented Christmas*, Broadway Books (New York, NY) 2008

Tomalin, Claire, *Charles Dickens: A Life*, The Penguin Press (New York, NY) 2011

Tomalin, Claire, *The Invisible Woman*, Knopf (New York, NY) 1991

Topham, Edward, *The Life of the Late John Elwes, Esquire*, Paraclete Potter (Poughkeepsie, NY) 1790

Tyler, Daniel, *A Guide to Dickens London*, Hesperus Press (London, England) 2012

Wagenknecht, Edward, *Dickens and the Scandalmongers*, University of Oklahoma Press (Norman, OK) 1965

Watkin, Edward William, *Canada and the States Recollections 1851 to 1886*

Wilkie, Katherine E., *Charles Dickens: The Inimitable Boz*, Abelard-Shuman (New York, NY) 1970

Wilson, Angus, *The World of Charles Dickens*, The Viking Press (New York, NY) 1970

N/A Ebenezer Scrooge, Historium.com, http://historum.com/blogs/chookie/580-ebeneezer-scrooge.html

N/A, "Sketcher, Tea & Coffee," *The Kyabram Union and Rodney Shire Advocate* (Vic.: 1894–1894) July 20, 1894

N/A, "Revealed: the Scot who inspired Dickens' Scrooge," *The Scotsman* (Edinburgh, Scotland) April 24, 2014

Photography Credits

Page 9 wikipedia

Page 11 Courtesy of Gerald Dickens

Page 16 wikipedia

Page 18 wikipedia

Page 23 wikipedia

Page 31 "Portrait of Frances Elizabeth Dickens ("Fanny Dickens") by Samuel Laurence. Photocopy of a drawing" Reproduced by Courtesy of Charles Dickens Museum, London

Page 45 Copyright Kim Traynor, wikipedia commons GNU license

Page 49 wikipedia

Page 80 wikipedia

Page 81 wikipedia

Page 102 Library of Congress

Page 108 wikipedi

Page 121 wikipedia

Page 136 wikipedia

Page 150 wikipedia

Page 163 wikipedia

Page 183 wikipedia

Page 209 wikipedia

Page 217 wikipedia

Page 225 wikipedia

Page 227 wikipedia

Page 228 Library of Congress

All chapter-opening art is from Shutterstock

About the Author

Carlo DeVito is the author of more than fifteen books including *A Mark Twain Christmas* and *10 Secrets My Dog Taught Me*. He is a longtime publishing executive and has published titles by Stephen Hawking, Dan Rather, Malachy McCourt, Haynes Johnson, and many other prominent authors. His own work as author and editor has been reviewed in *The Wall Street Journal*, *The Christian Science Monitor*, *USA Today*, the *Hartford Courant*, and others, and he's been featured on CBS, ABC, NBC, and FOX television and WFAN, WCBS, WABC, and ESPN radio, as well as many other TV and radio stations nationwide. He published the highly acclaimed book *Strange Fruit* by *Vanity Fair* contributing editor David Margolick, and is the inventor of the Mini Kit, which has millions in print worldwide. He is co-owner of the Hudson-Chatham Winery, and lives in Ghent, New York, with his family.